FOR DUMMIES™

BESTSELLING
BOOK SERIES

Computer Viruses
For Dummies

D1169383

Antivirus Configuration

- Whole-computer scan scheduled at least once weekly.
- Virus signature update scheduled at least once daily.
- Real-time virus detection turned on.
- Heuristic virus detection turned on.
- E-mail message scanning — inbound *and* outbound — turned on.

Antivirus Chores

Daily

- Check to make sure your antivirus program is running by checking the system tray for the antivirus program icon.

Weekly

- Scan your entire computer for viruses, and confirm that the scan has completed. Check the status to see if any infected files were found. If you're running scans automatically, check to make sure it actually ran.
- Make sure that your virus signature files have been updated.

How to Scan for Viruses

- Double-click or right-click the Antivirus System Tray icon; navigate to scan, and go!
- In Windows Explorer, right-click file or directory and select Scan.

If a Virus Is Found on Your Computer

- Read the alert carefully to see if the virus has been removed. Note the name of the file and the name of the virus. Go to your antivirus company's Web site for more information.
- See if a virus removal tool or other procedure is necessary to completely clean your computer.
- Update your virus signature files right away.
- Scan your entire computer for viruses.

For Dummies: Bestselling Book Series for Beginners

Computer Viruses For Dummies®

Safe-Computing Tips

- Never open e-mail messages from people you do not know.
- Never open attachments in unexpected or strange messages from people you don't know (or do know).
- Install security patches when they are available.
- Turn on Automatic Updates so that you can learn of new security patches when they become available (Windows 2000 and Windows XP only).
- Regularly back up your important data.
- Use secure Web browser settings.
- Download files only from trusted and well-known sites.
- Use alternate e-mail accounts for higher risk activities like mailing lists and Web site registrations.
- Disconnect your computer from the Internet when you are not using it.
- Password protect and use your screen saver if you work where others have access to your computer.
- Filter annoying and harmful e-mail with a spam filtering program.
- Block worms and Trojan horses with a hardware or software firewall.
- Block spyware and other potentially harmful software with a spyware filtering program.
- Don't go to Web sites you've never heard of before.

Where to Go for Security Information

- U.S. Computer Emergency Response Team: www.cert.org
- Microsoft Security Web Site: www.microsoft.com/security
- Microsoft Windows Update: windowsupdate.microsoft.com

For Dummies: Bestselling Book Series for Beginners

Computer Viruses FOR DUMMIES®

by Peter Gregory

WILEY

Wiley Publishing, Inc.

Computer Viruses For Dummies®

Published by
Wiley Publishing, Inc.
111 River Street
Hoboken, NJ 07030-5774

Copyright © 2004 by Wiley Publishing, Inc., Indianapolis, Indiana

Published by Wiley Publishing, Inc., Indianapolis, Indiana

Published simultaneously in Canada

For general information on our other products and services or to obtain technical support, please contact our Customer Care Department within the U.S. at 800-762-2974, outside the U.S. at 317-572-3993, or fax 317-572-4002.

Wiley also publishes its books in a variety of electronic formats. Some content that appears in print may not be available in electronic books.

Library of Congress Control Number: 2004107888

ISBN: 0-7645-7418-3

Manufactured in the United States of America

10 9 8 7 6 5 4 3 2

10/RQ/QY/QU/IN

WILEY

About the Author

Peter H. Gregory, CISA, CISSP, discovered computers in 1976 in his first year at the University of Nevada-Reno. He was taking a FORTRAN programming course when computer programs were painstakingly typed in on punch cards (hanging chads and all). He then got a part-time computer operator job at the University computer center, where he operated the university's mainframe computer, a Control Data Corporation CDC-6400. His insatiable curiosity about computers led him headlong into a career that began when he completed his university education.

Those fancy letters behind Peter's name: CISSP and CISA, are two professional security certifications: Certified Information Systems Security Professional and Certified Information Systems Auditor. Peter has spent the past eleven years in the wireless telecommunications industry, working in positions where he develops security policy, security architecture, security emergency response teams, and has been a security consultant in general. His love for personal computers has kept him attached to one or more of them for twenty years.

Author's Acknowledgments

I would like to extend thanks to great folks at Trend Micro (Michael Sweeny in the U.S. and Del Gemmell in Taiwan) and Panda Software (Alan Wallace in California, Jose Javier Merchan, and especially Fernando de la Cuadra in Spain), who provided information as well as dozens of screen shots. Special thanks go to Jennifer Byrne at Symantec who provided invaluable feedback on the draft table of contents, resulting in numerous improvements. Nalleli Lopez Hosek and David Alderman read the entire draft manuscript and made numerous productive suggestions to make the book easier to read and understand. Thanks you two! Tim Crothers worked hard to ensure the technical accuracy of the book.

Special thanks go to Eva Neumann, who provided invaluable feedback from her perspective as a non-professional computer user. Many thanks to my immediate and extended family for tolerating the book writing process yet again. I'd like to dedicate this book to the memory of Ralph Pratt who showed me how to teach complex subjects to non-technical people.

And thanks be to God, through whom all things are possible.

Publisher's Acknowledgments

We're proud of this book; please send us your comments through our online registration form located at www.dummies.com/register/.

Some of the people who helped bring this book to market include the following:

Acquisitions, Editorial, and Media Development

Project Editor: Kyle Looper

Acquisitions Editor: Melody Layne

Copy Editor: Barry Childs-Helton

Technical Editor: Tim Crothers

Editorial Manager: Leah P. Cameron

Media Development Manager: Laura VanWinkle

Media Development Supervisor: Richard Graves

Editorial Assistant: Amanda Foxworth

Cartoons: Rich Tennant (www.the5thwave.com)

Production

Project Coordinator: Courtney MacIntyre

Layout and Graphics: Andrea Dahl, Lauren Goddard, Denny Hager, Joyce Haughey, Michael Kruzil, Jacque Schneider

Proofreaders: Carl William Pierce, TECHBOOKS Production Services

Indexer: TECHBOOKS Production Services

Special Help Dru Hoskins

Publishing and Editorial for Technology Dummies

Richard Swadley, Vice President and Executive Group Publisher

Andy Cummings, Vice President and Publisher

Mary Bednarek, Executive Acquisitions Director

Mary C. Corder, Editorial Director

Publishing for Consumer Dummies

Diane Graves Steele, Vice President and Publisher

Joyce Pepple, Acquisitions Director

Composition Services

Gerry Fahey, Vice President of Production Services

Debbie Stailey, Director of Composition Services

Contents at a Glance

Table of Contents

Introduction

● ●

*I*t would be difficult to describe the impact of viruses — and their cousins Trojan horses and worms — without resorting to clichés or sensationalism. But after all the hoopla, the bottom line is pretty simple: Malicious people write viruses, and viruses do bad things to our computers. Over the past two decades, viruses have caused *billions* of dollars in damage and lost productivity — and that's just the impact on *businesses*. Viruses hit home computer users much harder because home users usually don't have information-technology support departments to install and maintain antivirus software and repair damaged computers.

But viruses *can* be stopped before they stop us, *and it's not hard to stop them.* Getting antivirus software is part of the solution. Using antivirus software is just a matter of doing a few simple chores to make sure that everything is working correctly: the better antivirus programs available today do all the regular tasks *automatically,* and only rarely do they require you to do something special.

If the information on your computer is important to you, then it's worth protecting. You can do several things to help protect your computer and the information stored in it. The Internet is not exactly a friendly place; in fact it can be quite hostile and unforgiving to those who are unable to protect themselves. But since you have either purchased or borrowed this book, you're on the verge of being able to get rid of the viruses on your computer and keep them away for good. It's all within your grasp!

About This Book

Computer Viruses For Dummies is a reference book, not (believe it or not) a mystery; you don't have to read the chapters in order. Start anywhere you like. Feel free to skip chapters that aren't of immediate interest. Want to start at the last page? You're the boss; everybody knows who done it anyway — that sinister virus.

If you're looking for particular information, you can go about it in several ways. You can use the Table of Contents to find the area of immediate interest. Or, you can look at the Index to find a particular word or concept. Finally, at the top of each page, a running head tells you what chapter and what part of the book you're currently in. Feel free to just skip around until you find the information you seek . . . unless you already have the queasy feeling that your computer may be infected. Then your best bet is to "start at the beginning" (as Lewis Carroll recommends) and explore from there.

How This Book Is Organized

This book is divided into five parts so you can find the information you need to find — quickly. Here's a rundown of each part:

Part 1: Evaluating Your Virus Situation

This part describes the risk factors associated with contracting computer viruses, ranging from your computing patterns to whether you take the time to install security patches and whether you have antivirus software. Next you'll read the steps to take to determine whether your computer has a virus, and whether your computer has properly functioning antivirus software.

Part 11: Deploying Your Antivirus Defenses

This is an action-filled part. Here you get a look at where to shop for antivirus software — and what features to look for (sorry, no bevawatt lasers for vaporizing virus writers, but hey, we can dream). I won't tell you which brand to buy — I'd rather help you be a good shopper than pick stuff for you that may not be what you need. After installing your antivirus software, there are important steps to take to make sure it performs all the necessary steps to protect your computer and your information. Next, you go on a virus hunt, scanning your computer for viruses and going through the steps that actually remove a virus if one is found.

Part III: Maintaining Your Vigilance

"Eternal vigilance is the price of liberty," said a distinguished figure from American history whose name I forget just now. One modern equivalent is "Eternal updating is the price of security." Antivirus software isn't a magical guardian; you can't just install it and then forget it (sorry). Keeping your antivirus software up to date is what keeps it effective. In addition, this part looks at some other wise practices that are also vital to long-term safe computing, for example:

- ✔ Installing security patches and service packs
- ✔ Backing up your data
- ✔ Blocking spam and spyware
- ✔ Using a hardware or software firewall
- ✔ Being smart about not opening certain messages and about avoiding certain Web sites

If you own a PDA and keep *everything* in it, this part also offers some safe practices you can adopt to keep your PDA useful and your data available — and only for you.

Part IV: Looking at Viruses Under the Microscope

The more you know about viruses and the people who write them, the better you can protect yourself against them. Viruses got their start in the 1980s, soon after the introduction of the IBM PC. Since then they have evolved and grown more sophisticated. Other threats such as Trojan horses, worms, scams, and hoaxes add to the challenge of keeping our computers free from harm and saving us from unnecessary worry and distraction.

Part V: The Part of Tens

Do you like lists and statistics? Do you want more insight into viruses and the tools that repel them? This is the place! You'll find popular myths about viruses debunked, and common questions answered. Ten popular antivirus programs are examined — tools for doing battle with the next round of notorious viruses.

Conventions Used in This Book

When you need to issue a command in Windows, I show a command like this: Tools➪Options. In this example, click Tools from the menu bar at the top of the window, then click Options from the list. If you don't see Options in the list, you might need to press the double-arrow at the bottom of the list of options to make all the options appear.

When there is a command like Ctrl+Q, do it like this: Hold down either one of the Ctrl keys, and while still holding it down, press and release the Q key, then release the Ctrl key. The Ctrl key works just like a Shift key.

What You're Not to Read

. . . unless, of course, you find 'em interesting . . . are the gray boxes (called *sidebars*) and icons that denote technical information. They're dribbled throughout this book; you can feel free to skip these treatises at will. Some actually have some interesting information, though, so feel free to read 'em anyway. If I really felt that you didn't need to know this stuff, I would have left it out of the book. Honest.

Meanings of the Term "Virus"

Most of the time I discuss three different types of threats in this book: viruses, Trojan horses, and worms. In Part IV, I describe each species in grisly detail.

I use the term *virus* constantly throughout this book — as an inclusive term that includes viruses, Trojan horses, and worms — or (depending on the context) to mean only a virus. (Only?) There's still some argument going on among computer-security professionals regarding what, exactly, a virus *is* (does it always have to work like those tiny semiliving things that give you a cold?). But the intent of malicious code is always clear.

Foolish Assumptions

Okay, so I'm going to start by telling you who I think you are, so you can find out whether I have a future in fortunetelling. Wait, I'm getting something . . . (now mind you, this works better if I can have something personal of yours — a $100 bill works best — to hold while I concentrate):

- You know — or fear — that your computer has a virus, and you don't know what to do.

- Like 97 percent of the computer world, you use Windows as your operating system.

- You use your computer at home for entertainment, Web surfing, and maybe as a part of your profession. Maybe all three.

- You want to know how much at risk you are, and if you're properly protected.

- You want to know more about how to use your antivirus program.

- You want to move beyond antivirus software and begin to learn about antispyware and firewalls.

- You have a PDA and are interested in protecting it from viruses.

- You want to seek revenge against all the virus writers in the world.

- Or, maybe someone gave you this book and, although you don't have a clue what all this virus stuff is about, you figure that it might make a good beach read.

This is who I think you're *not:*

- ✔ **You're probably not a network administrator:** Although understanding viruses and virus protection are of utmost importance to the security of any enterprise network and understanding the concepts in this book is important to system administrators, this book is geared toward end users.

- ✔ **You're probably not a Linux or Mac user:** Viruses hit both of these operating systems, just like they hit Windows, but this book concentrates primarily on the Windows operating system.

- ✔ **You're probably not a virus writer:** This book provides *zero* information on how to write or distribute viruses. If you're a virus writer, please put this book down right now and get a life instead.

- ✔ **You're obviously no dummy:** And you're not a mark either. Even if you don't know a thing about computer viruses, buying this book shows just how smart you are. After reading this book, the virus writers will have to look elsewhere for prey, and your friends might turn to *you* for advice.

The use of good protective software does not give you license to be irresponsible. Even with a good antivirus program, a fire-wall, and spyware blockers, you still need to practice safe computing. Some of the things that can go wrong transcend the ability of protective software to save you from good old (actually *bad* old) human error. You still need to be careful! I dedicate an entire chapter on being careful — that's how important good computer hygiene is.

Icons Used in This Book

If you've used Windows or the graphical interface for Unix, you've seen icons. They're the little symbols that appear on the screen that have special meaning. I use icons in this book, too, and they're a lot easier to understand than the ones used in Windows:

Here is a shortcut or hint to save you time or trouble.

Get out your geeky glasses, plaid shirt, and pocket protector!

Watch out! Some trap or pitfall awaits you.

Don't forget these important points — they are well worth, uh, remembering!

Where to Go from Here

You don't need to be a computer scientist or have a Ph.D. to be able to stop viruses. You need only a few basic skills, and I'll show you how to do all the basic things to get rid of viruses and keep them away for good. If you want to understand the big picture of fighting computer viruses, then you can start at Chapter 1. If (on the other hand) you want to know *right now* whether your computer is infected with a virus, go straight to Chapter 2.

Of course, you can also feel free to start wherever the heck you want. This book allows you to chart your own course through the virus jungle.

If you want to arm yourself with additional Windows PC skills and knowledge, pick up one of the following (each by Andy Rathbone):

- *Windows XP For Dummies*
- *Windows 2000 For Dummies*
- *Windows 98 For Dummies*

If you want to get a line on protecting your online privacy and security, try one or more of these:

- *Fighting Spam For Dummies,* by John Levine, Margaret Levine-Young, and Ray Everett-Church
- *Internet Privacy For Dummies,* by John Levine, Ray Everett-Church, and Greg Stebben

    ✔ *PCs For Dummies,* 9th Edition, by Dan Gookin

    ✔ *Wireless Home Networking For Dummies,* by Danny Briere, Pat Hurley, and Walter Bruce

Write to Us!

Have a question? Comment? Complaint? Please let me know. Write to me at

```
questions@computervirusesbook.com
```

You'll get an automatic response with some helpful information. I'll *try* to answer every question personally. Or, look for the <u>Frequently-Asked Questions</u> link at

```
www.computervirusesbook.com
```

For information on other *For Dummies* books, please visit

```
www.dummies.com
```

Part I

Evaluating Your Virus Situation

"OH YEAH, AND TRY NOT TO ENTER THE WRONG PASSWORD."

In this part . . .

*M*any factors contribute to the likelihood that your computer will get infected with a virus. Your handling of e-mail messages from people you don't know is one of the biggest factors, as is the general health of your antivirus software.

Does your computer have a virus — right now? Wouldn't you like to know?! Some symptoms may indicate a virus, but other symptoms probably don't. By performing a simple procedure, you can determine this reliably. If you have a virus, a couple more steps and ZAP, it's gone. And with relative ease, you can eliminate any spyware on your computer, too.

Many computing habits are associated with a far lower risk of getting infected by computer viruses and other similar trouble. Among them are keeping your antivirus software up to date and periodically installing security patches.

The first important task to virus-free computing is to check whether your computer has antivirus software, and if so, whether it's in good condition or not. There are a number of ways to tell whether antivirus software is present, and whether its basic components are functioning correctly.

Chapter 1

Understanding Virus Risks

*T*here's an old saying: "Just because you're not paranoid doesn't mean that everyone isn't out to get you." This saying is proven by the people who write computer viruses — they *are* out to get you! And, in fact, a little paranoia may go a long way in protecting your computer.

In this chapter, I provide you with the factors that may increase your personal level of useful paranoia — in other words, the factors that can influence you to lower your personal risk level. Why? Because, get this, some people are more apt to catch computer viruses than others, and it's largely based upon some basic factors such as the version of Windows they're using, as well as their Internet and e-mail habits. In the computer world as well as in the biological world, good hygiene goes a long way in preventing infection in the first place — and prevention is far easier to deal with than curing an infection after it happens.

Assessing the Threat to Your Computer

Three primary factors contribute to your risk of catching viruses:

- ✔ The version of the Windows operating system you are using
- ✔ Whether you have installed security patches on your computer
- ✔ How many people use the computer

But also important are your Internet browsing habits:

- ✔ Do you visit many different Web sites?
- ✔ Do you visit sites that try to mess with your computer's settings (and how would you know — and prevent — that)?
- ✔ Do you have a tendency to open e-mail attachments from people you don't know?
- ✔ Do you visit Web sites cited in e-mail messages from strangers?

All these factors have a direct bearing on whether you are prone to catching viruses.

Finally, the manner in which your computer is connected to the Internet determines your susceptibility to viruses. If you have a high-speed, "always-on" Internet connection, then virus writers are actively trying to find you (or already have!). Dial-up connections are *somewhat* less risky — but not risk-free.

Which operating system are you using?

Microsoft's earlier versions of Windows had very little in the way of security — they conformed to Microsoft's earlier (and flawed) premise that everyone in corporations and everyone on the Internet is nice and can be trusted and that no one will do anything bad. Microsoft, by the way, has been humbled by the experience and, as a result, the newer versions of Windows are far more secure than their predecessors.

Windows 95 and Windows 98

Collectively known as Windows 9*x,* these earlier versions of Windows lack the basic security components found in modern operating systems. Their primary fault is that they don't separate the function of the operating system from the person who uses it. You, the computer's user, have complete control over every aspect of the computer. Even back in the '90s that wasn't too safe; if you catch a virus, *the virus has the same range of control over your computer as you do.*

Microsoft no longer supports Windows 95. This means that, if any security vulnerability is discovered in Windows 95, Microsoft will not issue bulletins, advice, or security patches to fix it. Not an enviable position for any user to be in.

In 2003, Microsoft announced that it would soon end support for Windows 98. But when thousands of corporate and individual computer users stormed the Microsoft castle in Redmond, Washington, armed with torches, spears, axes, and old dot-matrix printers, Microsoft relented and postponed the Windows 98 "end of life."

But for users of Windows 98, the message is clear: Your days of support from Microsoft are growing short.

Windows ME

Officially called Windows Millennium Edition or Windows ME (and playfully referred to in some circles as the Windows Miserable Edition), this is just Windows 98 with some additional features thrown in and some stability improvements. The stability improvements come at the price of higher hardware requirements, however, and Windows ME suffers from the same basic security issues as its predecessors, namely that viruses can run roughshod throughout the unprotected operating system.

Windows 2000

At long last, Microsoft had taken the kernel (insides) of Windows NT and grafted on the Windows 98 *user interface* (the stuff that you see on-screen when you use it), and after exhausting the world's supply of duct tape and baling wire, made it work.

Windows 2000 is a very decent operating system. It contains most of the security features that corporate customers and consumers had been requesting for a long time. Primary is the notion of "logging on" to the computer. In Windows 2000 and newer versions of Windows, if you can't log on to the computer, you can't use it. Contrast that to Windows 9*x* — if you can make the computer run, you can use it and do anything you want to it.

Windows XP

Windows XP contains many refinements over Windows 2000 and is even more secure. For the most part, Windows XP is an improved version of Windows 2000 and includes additional features and functions.

I've heard some say that Windows XP is just Windows 2000 with the soft, friendly interface. If you haven't seen Windows XP, it's like Windows 2000 with brighter colors and smooth, rounded corners.

Do you install security patches?

Microsoft regularly releases *security patches* — fixes to their software — that close security holes that could lead to virus infections. Many of these patches are deemed "critical," and a good number of them have been exploited by those chip-on-their-shoulder Internet thugs who have nothing better to do than to spread misery to as many people as possible.

Microsoft has provided a number of ways that you can use to find out about and install security patches, including Windows Update, Automatic Update, and e-mail notifications of new patches.

If you *do* install the critical patches that Microsoft releases, then you're in far better shape than if you have no security patches at all. Having no security patches is almost as bad as having no antivirus software: You're up the creek with a sitting duck.

I don't want you to feel bad if you're among (what I suspect is) the majority of computer users — those who have never installed security patches. Had I chosen a different career path without much chance to get familiar with computers, the thought of installing security patches would seem about as intimidating as working on my home's electrical wiring or working on a late-model automobile with all its complex wiring and safety systems. But that's what this book is for: to help get you past the reluctance.

How many people use the computer?

Are you the only person who uses your computer? Or are several colleagues, family members, or (gasp!) total strangers using your computer, like so many people sharing a germ-infested bathroom water cup?

The greater the number of people using a computer, the greater the chances are that something bad will happen. How do I know this? When several people share a complex machine like a PC, the inconsistencies in the ways that the people use the computer, and the accumulation of every user's bad habits and mistakes, can make the computer's condition deteriorate over time.

How is your computer connected to the Internet?

While there are many ways to connect to the Internet, I'm concerned with just one factor: Is your computer "always on and connected" through any sort of a *broadband* (high-speed) connection like DSL, a cable modem, ISDN, or satellite? Or do you use a dial-up (phone-line) connection to connect your computer to the Internet, get your e-mail, do a little surfing, and then disconnect?

It boils down to this: Is your computer *always on* and *always connected* to the Internet? If so, then your computer is far more likely to be targeted by Internet worms. Some hackers like to scan for — and find — new always-on computers.

They're looking for recruits — to see whether they can add your system to their legion of slave computers.

Let me explain this high-speed, always-on thing a little more. If your computer is connected to the Internet using a high-speed connection, then your computer is *statistically* more likely to be found by a scan than it would be if it were connected, say, only one or two hours per day. Statistically speaking, an always-on computer is ten times more likely to be scanned, because it's connected ten times as many hours per day. But more than that, if your computer is always on and always connected, then hackers would consider your computer more dependable. And because the connection is higher speed than dial-up, they can get more performance out of your computer for their own evil purposes.

Do you have a firewall?

A firewall, as I explain more fully in Chapter 10, is something that is designed to block the probing scans that are often associated with viruses, worms, and Trojan horses. Those people who have installed either a software firewall or a hardware firewall have far better protection than people who have neither.

A *software firewall* is a program that runs on your computer, invisibly (in the background), much like an antivirus program. The software firewall program carefully watches all communication coming into your computer and leaving your computer. Each network message — or *packet* — is examined to ascertain its type, origin, and destination. These properties are then compared to a list of rules to determine whether each packet should be allowed to pass through or not. Should the message be allowed to pass, the firewall lets it move along towards its destination. But should the message be blocked, then the firewall will not permit it to pass — and it will fail to reach its destination, like a postal letter that is intercepted in transit and simply thrown away.

A *hardware firewall* is an electronic appliance that is installed on a network. Its internal function is essentially similar to the software firewall, except that its protection is more centralized: All the computers on the network are protected by the hardware firewall, so none of the bad traffic on the Internet is permitted to reach any of the computers on the network.

The legion of zombies

Many of the viruses, worms, and Trojan horses that have been released in recent years have a single, diabolical purpose — to identify and "take over" those so-called always-on and always-connected computers that are typically connected to the Internet using high-speed DSL, cable modem, ISDN, or satellite connections.

A recent study estimates that fully *one-third* of all such computers have *backdoors* (programs that allow hackers to bypass all security) installed on them and are used for a variety of purposes — generally for transmitting spam (unwanted junk) e-mail or for participating in massive distributed denial of service (DDoS) attacks.

A *distributed denial of service* (DDoS) attack is one where a hacker, after enlisting hundreds or thousands of computers with his backdoor program, sends a command to "his" (your) computer, instructing it (and many, many others) to begin flooding some particular Web site with as many network messages as possible. The victim's Web site would then be receiving millions of network messages from hundreds or thousands of computers located all over the world and be nearly powerless to stop it (because of the vast number of sources of the attack). As a result, the victim's Web site would, for all

practical purposes, be "off the air" for as long as the attack continued.

This is no pipe dream or theoretical missive. Such attacks are commonplace. Major corporations, organizations, and governments, such as Microsoft, SCO, Yahoo!, E-Trade, the U.S. Whitehouse, and some countries' government or news sites, have been victims of DDoS attacks lasting hours or days. And unless that corporation is both clever and resourceful, the corporation's Web site is essentially unreachable for all legitimate use until the attack ceases.

Home users — even those who are IT professionals by day — would likely have no reason to suspect that their home PCs have been taken over. Generally speaking, hackers have designed their backdoors to minimize the likelihood of being detected. They use a measured, limited portion of your computer's resources so you can continue to use your computer for whatever you do with it. At the same time, however, your computer would also be used to relay and transmit spam to hundreds or thousands of other unsuspecting people (and many of *those* spam messages may contain their own viruses, worms, or Trojan horses to enlist even more unsuspecting and poorly-protected computers). Your computer could be the modern version of the zombies in *Night of the Living Dead*.

A firewall is like a security guard at the entrance of an office building. He (or she) scrutinizes each person coming and going. He may want to look at each person's identification by examining their employee badge or other credential. If the person coming or going is carrying anything, he may ask questions about it. If the person is a guest, the guard may request that the user sign their name into a visitor's log.

The guard has a list of rules that he uses to determine whether each person coming and going will be permitted to pass through. Occasionally he will need to turn someone away, for one reason or another. He will detail each such denial so his boss can later view who was denied access and why.

Occasionally, the guard will need to call his boss and ask if a visitor is permitted to pass through (in a firewall software program, this takes the form of a pop-up window that asks if a particular program should be permitted to communicate or not).

High-risk activities

The types of activities performed on your PC also contribute to your risk, whether high or low. Each of these activities is related to how social you permit your computer to be. Do you often take it out in public where it can exchange information with other computers? In the analogy between biological viruses and computer viruses, a high degree of *socialization* (mingling with others) increases risk. The following sections look at some examples.

Wireless "Hot Spots"

Hoping to attract well-to-do customers, many public establishments — such as coffee houses, restaurants, and other businesses — have installed so-called Internet *hot spots*. These hot spots are Internet connections that a customer can use to connect to the Internet with a laptop computer, provided it's equipped with a wireless networking (also called Wi-Fi or 802.11) capability. Some establishments charge a fee for the use of their hot spots; others permit use free of charge.

People who own laptops equipped with those Wi-Fi connections can visit any of the hundreds of thousands (or perhaps millions) of Wi-Fi–equipped establishments and access the Internet to retrieve e-mail, visit Web sites, or whatever they do on the Internet. At a coffeehouse, for instance, you would purchase your tall double-shot vanilla low-fat latte and then sit down at one of the tables, turn on your laptop, and catch up on e-mail while quaffing your favorite coffee drink.

But here's the problem: These hot-spot connections have many of the same risks that are associated with always-on high-speed connections. Hackers and worms frequently scan the wireless networks in these establishments, hoping to find new victims — like, f'rinstance, your computer. Computers lacking adequate antivirus protection fall victim to the worm and become one of those zombie computers, awaiting the commands from their fiendish master.

Downloading and file sharing

If you or someone with access to your computer is doing a lot of file and program downloading and file sharing with others, chances are that sooner or later one of the files you download will be infected with a virus.

Because many viruses travel from computer to computer by hiding inside of software program files, it makes sense that the more program files you bring into your system, the more likely it will be that one of them will have a virus. Also, program files that have been copied from other computers (rather than coming directly from the manufacturer) have a *much* greater chance of being infected with a virus.

Instant messaging

If you are an Instant Messaging (IM) user, you are increasing your chances of catching a virus (or, of course a worm, Trojan, or other ill fate). As the popularity of IM rises, so too does this get the attention of virus writers looking for new ways to get viruses from one computer to another. Already, there have been a number of worms that have propagated themselves using IM. Every day, minute by minute, you can be sure that there will have been more such incidents.

Add-on programs

If you are the type who can't resist an online or computer store bargain, sooner or later something you pick up will have a little extra feature. While it doesn't happen often, viruses have been known to sneak onto the *gold* (or final) version of a software manufacturer's CD-ROM or online download area.

How many viruses are there?

Tens of thousands of viruses, worms, and Trojan horses have been developed and released onto the Internet over the past two decades. On the day that I am writing this section, my own PC's antivirus program shows over 66,000 known viruses in its list.

In the first half of 2003 alone, 3,855 new viruses were introduced. That is over 21 new viruses each and every day.

Nearly all new viruses are targeted at Microsoft products, including Windows, Outlook, and Office.

And remember — virus writers like to get their viruses to propagate in large numbers. That means, some spend considerable time trying to get their wares into programs that will be mass-marketed or mass-distributed.

Sharing your e-mail address with too many other people and organizations

Persons who have a habit of signing up for things on the Internet are far more likely to end up on one or more spammers' lists. Or if you are the type of person whose e-mail address is "in circulation" — meaning your e-mail address appears online in Web sites, chat rooms, mailing lists, newsgroups, and so forth — then the chances improve that your e-mail address will be picked up and wind up in the hands of one or more mass marketers. As soon as this happens, one or more of the spammers who like to send large volumes (we're talking *millions*) of virus-laden e-mail messages will take advantage of the target you've given them.

This is not unlike giving out your phone number to lots of different people and organizations, only to discover that you are beginning to receive far more unwanted phone calls than before. So it is with e-mail. It's the fastest possible way to infest your once-pristine inbox with more unwanted mail than legitimate mail.

In my case, about *three-fourths* of all the e-mail I receive is spam. My e-mail address appears in my online column in

ComputerWorld. Of course, the address I use there is different from any I use anywhere else — and it isn't hard to see why: Soon after I started writing my column, I began to receive additional spam, much of it sent to that unique address. This occurs because some spammers have *spider* programs that run all over the Web in search of e-mail addresses to harvest from Web sites.

Deciding How Much Security Is Enough

Without getting too scientific about it, the best way to think about "how much security is enough" is to compare the value of the possession you are trying to protect against the level of effort you're willing to expend to protect it.

Let me illustrate with a simple example. Would you protect a $1,000 automobile with a $2,000 alarm system? Not likely, because it isn't proportional.

Like shoes and bathing suits, one size does not fit all people and all needs. And so it is with computers. Depending on what you do with your computer, you will need to spend a particular level of effort in order to protect the information on your computer and the ability to continue performing whatever activities you use it for.

For example, a casual user sends and receives e-mail and surfs the Internet. But someone else uses their computer to make their living: Perhaps they use their computer to build Web sites, do financial accounting for small businesses, or write *For Dummies* books. The latter user has a lot more to lose if something goes wrong with his or her computer, than does the casual user, who is merely inconvenienced.

Take a look at three somewhat arbitrary levels of security in Table 1-1. Each one also represents a level of value, and I include examples of how often particular security activities should take place.

Table 1-1	Levels of Security		
Typical Uses	*Low*	*Medium*	*High*
	Casual e-mail, computer games, Web-surfing	Family or business correspondence, online bill payment	Small business accounting, writer of *For Dummies* books
Virus scans	Monthly	Weekly	Daily
Virus updates	Weekly	Daily	Hourly
Risk tolerance	High	Medium	Low
Backups	Infrequent	Weekly	Daily

You can see in these examples that the higher-value systems deserve more elaborate protection. If you think about it, a high-value system is helping its owner to derive income or some other economic value, or pursue some other form of value that the user feels personally invested in. Given the risks associated with online computing, it makes sense to protect systems associated with economic (or other) value more than systems that were little more than hobbyist-level systems.

Chapter 2

Does My Computer Have a Virus?

. . . .

In This Chapter

▶ Looking at common virus symptoms

▶ Finding and fixing a virus

▶ Developing good habits

▶ Finding out more about viruses

. . . .

Does your computer have a virus? Or are you just *afraid* that your computer has a virus? Either way, you've come to the right place. If your computer has started to act funny — if it just doesn't *feel* right — then it's possible (but not certain) that your computer has a virus.

This chapter gives you the information necessary to help you determine whether your computer has a virus, and then points you in the right direction to find out what to do next. Just remember this: Nobody *deserves* to get a computer virus.

If you *do* have a virus, batten down the hatches and brace for a fight — viruses are a pain in the neck at best, and they can be *much* worse. Armed with this book, however, you're in a much better position to come out victorious in a scrape with a virus (and to avoid being infected in the future).

Looking at Common Virus Symptoms

Stalking the wild computer virus starts with observation: There are a lot of ways that a computer can begin to act strangely for no apparent reason. These changes in behavior may be the result of a virus, but there are other possible explanations as well.

This section describes some typical virus-induced symptoms, as well as some ways to determine whether a virus is responsible for your computer's symptoms.

Computer too slow

The first thing to check when your computer is slow is to make sure that your computer isn't in a school zone. Seriously, a slowing in your computer can be the result of a number of circumstances — and a virus is definitely among them. The following list provides some considerations for making an educated guess as to why your computer is slowing down:

- **Have you made any changes to your computer lately?** For instance, have you upgraded to Windows 2000 or Windows XP? These newer operating systems require a lot more memory than their predecessors.

- **Have you upgraded a program?** Like Windows 2000 and Windows XP, newer versions of many other programs like Microsoft Office and Microsoft Works require a lot more memory than earlier versions.

- **Have you or a loved one downloaded a lot of "nature" pictures or other information?** Pictures and music take up space. If your hard drive is almost full, your computer will definitely run slower.

If you're sure you haven't made any changes, then you *may* have a virus. You'll have to check your computer's behavior and run a number of simple tests before you can be sure.

Unexplained activity

Does your hard-drive or network-activity light flicker for no apparent reason? While there may be a legitimate reason for it, this could also be a sign that a virus or a hacker's *back-door program* (a devious little program that allows secret access without your permission) is running on your computer. You might be donating some of your computer resources to a hacker and be largely unaware of it. Here are some examples of what could be going on if a hacker has gotten control of your computer:

- ✔ The hacker could be using your computer to send thousands, even millions, of those annoying spam messages to people all over the Internet.

- ✔ The hacker could be using your computer to launch attacks on corporate computing networks. In a DDoS (distributed denial of service) attack, for example, a hacker instructs thousands of "zombie" computers (like yours, perhaps) to send lots of messages to a particular corporate Web site, glutting its communications and knocking it off the Internet.

- ✔ The hacker could be using your computer to *scan* other networks, hunting for vulnerable *ports* (communication channels for particular computer processes) that can mean more potential-victim computers.

- ✔ The hacker may have installed spyware that reports back to the bad guys without the victim's (your) knowledge. One example is a *key logger* — a small program that records every key press and mouse movement in an attempt to learn your bank-account numbers, credit-card numbers, and other sensitive information that you probably don't want strangers to know about. (For more about this insidious stuff, see "Blocking spyware," later in this chapter.)

Crashes or hangs

Does your computer crash often? Does it just stop responding? Do you often get the Blue Screen of Death™? Again, there are many possible explanations. No cop-out, just reality. (Hey, if I had a crystal ball, I'd quit writing, buy office space on Bourbon Street in New Orleans, and make my fortune, right?)

Crashing, hanging, and blue screens may be virus-induced, but they're probably not. These maladies are more likely the result of new software, new drivers, or even a hardware component that's beginning to fail. Check out those possibilities first.

Will not boot

Boot used to be a noun — the leather thing you put on your foot to protect it from rough terrain. These days *boot* is a verb just as often; it's the process that your computer performs to start itself when you turn it on or press Ctrl+Alt+Del (the "three-finger salute").

You guessed it — just because your computer won't boot, it doesn't *necessarily* mean that your computer has a virus. Maybe yes, maybe no. There are several other likely explanations — for example, a corrupted *master boot record* (the part of the hard drive that your computer uses to start up), or damage to an important file that your computer uses to start up.

If either of these was the case, you'd probably have to rebuild your computer's operating system and file system from scratch — not fun, even for the experts — and recovering any lost data could get dicey in a hurry. But you know, if you're running Windows and have to reinstall your computer's operating system, here are a couple of basic improvements to consider:

- ✔ What better time to upgrade to Windows 2000 or Windows XP (unless you're already running one of those)?

- ✔ What better excuse to curl up with a good book — say, whichever *Windows For Dummies* book covers your newly installed version? This could be the perfect opportunity to read up on Windows while you're waiting for the install to finish.

Strange computer behavior

Okay, computers sometimes behave inscrutably, but their behavior should be predictable. Same deal for viruses — which means they can't *completely* conceal their activities.

You can look for the devil in the details. Perhaps the signs are obvious (the colors go all weird, the computer puts words on-screen by itself, or it makes strange noises) or relatively subtle (your screen borders pinch inward for an instant just before you send e-mail). Time to observe closely and take notes. For openers, consider some "obvious" symptoms:

✔ **Files are not where you left them, and can't be found on your computer.** If your computer has become a Bermuda Triangle that is eating your files, even some of your software, you might have a virus.

✔ **You can find the file, but its size or date stamp is suspiciously different.** Viruses that infect program files may make the files bigger or smaller than they should be, or change their date stamps. Date stamps don't ordinarily change on program files — ever — unless an official software patch changes them. Uh-oh.

✔ **On-screen text starts to change by itself.** In the old days of the DOS command prompt, one virus made the letters in on-screen text seem to move around "by themselves." Sometimes they changed colors, or started consuming each other like Pac-Man. Bad sign. But you knew that.

✔ **An out-of-context message appears on-screen.** Some viruses announce their presence by taunting the user. If you are greeted with a message such as `Your computer is now Stoned!`, you probably have a virus. Consider whether the message is out of context — for example, does it look like someone's trying to cap a practical joke with a punch line? Not funny at all.

These are just a few examples of the weird things a virus can do to your computer. Those virus writers are pretty creative (in an ugly sort of way).

Too many pop-up windows

While I can't prove it, I'd suspect that in some cases, Web sites that flood you with pop-up windows could also be attempting to download some malicious program(s) into your computer. Web sites that pump pop-ups into people's computers are notorious for *attempting to change the configuration of your Web browser* and other parts of your computer — by remote control, without your knowledge or permission.

Finding and Fixing a Virus

There are some tools and procedures that can tell with 99.44 percent accuracy whether your computer has a virus. Here are the actions to take:

✔ **Find out whether your computer has antivirus software:** Use Chapter 3 to help you find that out. If the steps in Chapter 3 lead you to believe that your computer does *not* have antivirus software, use Chapter 4 to help you obtain and install some.

✔ **Find out whether your antivirus software is up to date:** If you already have antivirus software installed on your computer, Chapter 9 can help you figure out whether it's up to date and working properly.

✔ **Scan your computer for viruses:** When you know that your computer has antivirus software — and that it's up to date — you can use it to scan your computer for viruses. Chapter 6 describes what to expect from this scan.

If you have an Internet connection, you might think that you can take a shortcut and try one of those online virus-scanning tools — but *don't do that at this point!* The risks of connecting to the Internet *without antivirus software and a firewall* are greater than the benefit you'd get from knowing whether you have a virus — and you could end up with a virus if you use the 'Net unprotected. (It's like drinking unboiled water from a polluted river — think Montezuma's Revenge here.)

For some really good reasons not to use an online scanning tool as a first resort, go to Chapters 6 through 10, where I explain local scanning, online scanning, and firewalls. (Chapter 10 goes into detail about firewalls.) Suffice to say: Make sure you're protected before you venture out.

✔ **Remove the virus:** If your virus-scanning tool finds a virus on your computer, Chapter 7 explains how to get rid of the ugly thing. There are two basic outcomes:

• **Automatic removal:** Chances are your virus-scanning tool will be able to fix your computer by removing the virus. Most of the time this is the case. Newer virus tools will, in effect, tell you, "Hey you, I found a virus on your computer. Do you want me to clean it up or not?" I really cannot imagine why you would want to say no.

Personally I think you should just get rid of the virus right away and deal with the consequences, however mild or severe, afterward.

- **Manual removal — and more work:** If, however, your virus-scanning tool tells you that it cannot get rid of the virus, a little more work is in order. For instance, you may need to download a special virus-removal tool from your antivirus software vendor; such tools are sometimes built for specific, hard-to-remove viruses. (I also explain these sometimes-necessary extra steps in Chapter 8.)

When you get rid of viruses, you've made a good start. (Done? Who said anything about *done?*) Review the ways you use your computer: Did something you do regularly get you into virus trouble in the first place? By identifying the things you do that expose you to threats like viruses, you can reduce your exposure by doing some things differently. Preventive actions — the cyber equivalent of washing your hands before handling food — take a little time, but they can save a lot of misery later.

Developing Good Habits

People remember their firsts — the first time driving a car, first kiss, first surgery, first computer virus. (Well, okay, some firsts *are* better than others — but most are memorable.) In the case of *this* first, here's something to keep in mind. . . .

If you got a computer virus, human error was probably a factor. Somebody probably wasn't doing something right. That, or you were extremely unlucky.

Nobody's exempt from human error (well, maybe chimpanzees). You may have opened an infected attachment by mistake, or missed out on the latest antivirus update. Or your friend who helped set up your computer may have skipped a step or left the wrong default in place. However it happened, you need to discover where the error came from. If you're like most people, you may be able to safeguard your computer by changing some habits. Those changes take two forms:

- ✔ Stopping virus-prone habits that put you at risk
- ✔ Starting some virus-savvy habits that make you less of a target

Having good, up-to-date antivirus software is essential. But there are some other good defensive tools such as firewalls and antispyware. In addition to these nice defensive tools, you may still have some old habits to break and new habits to take up.

The first good thing you did was buy this book. Now if you read carefully and take my advice to heart, you'll be much safer in the long run. (And don't forget to eat your vegetables.)

Keeping antivirus software up to date

Antivirus software is of little value if it's not kept up to date. One of those big-ego computer scientists once said that out-of-date antivirus software is as bad as having none at all. (Hey, sometimes the scientists *are* right.) The best antivirus program is next to useless if it's not kept up to date.

I show you how to keep your antivirus software current in Chapter 8. This is required reading, unless you want to catch more viruses in the future (hey, the virus writers would *love* you, but trust me, they won't respect you in the morning).

Scan for viruses periodically

Although rare, some viruses can sneak onto a computer without being detected at the time of their arrival. It's a very good idea to scan your entire computer for viruses from time to time — say, once a week. Read Chapter 6 to see how to set this up; chances are your antivirus program can do this automatically for you.

Install security patches

Security patches are fixes that software companies make to protect the computer programs they make from the villains who try to harm your computer. (Yes, Virginia, there really are people in the world who want to hurt other people and their property. But you knew that.)

Some patches fix malfunctions that sometimes crop up as a result of flaws in the product. If the flaws make your system vulnerable to hackers, the software maker creates patches that fix those specific vulnerabilities. Chapter 9 tells you more about security patches and why they're important. (For now, think about infestation, fumigation, and why malfunctions in computer programs are called "bugs.")

Working on good computer hygiene

In so many ways, it's a grubby Internet out there. You don't want to interact with it without protection. Fortunately, there's a wealth of good habits you can discover and adopt. They can be as effective (and simple) as washing your hands after using the bathroom. Used consistently, they can help keep you and your computer safe; I explain 'em in Chapter 12.

Blocking malicious network traffic with a firewall

In Chapter 10, I tell you a lot about firewalls. For now, consider this: You need one. Everybody needs one. Trust me on this.

Like antivirus software, *firewalls* protect your computer. Their function is to deflect the incoming bad things — viruses, worms, and Trojan horses — that antivirus software can't always stop. Having a firewall can help — a lot.

Blocking spyware

If you're like many of us, it isn't hard to get into the mood to give your computer a thorough cleaning — and I don't mean with spray disinfectant. Rather, I mean that it's time to go cloak-and-dagger and check for spyware on your computer.

Spyware can be a lot of things. In general, it's software that some Web sites and viruses install on your computer without your knowledge so some person or company can track your online movements, or even record your keystrokes with a key logger (also mentioned earlier in this chapter under "Strange computer behavior"). If it doesn't bother you that someone you don't know has knowledge about where you go on the Internet, then you don't need to know any more about spyware. But we're not talking Santa Claus here.

Many people in the United States and Europe find it repulsive to think that some total stranger knows about their Internet surfing habits. They don't *have* to have anything to hide — and most of the time, they don't. They just figure it's nobody else's business. I'm with them all the way.

Naturally, you can (and should) decide for yourself. But read Chapter 10 and see whether you want to better protect yourself with a spyware-detection tool.

Do you have a PDA?

If you have a Palm Pilot, a Pocket PC, or any of the other PDAs that are available, you should consider adopting some safe practices. It's a small computer, after all, and deserves to be kept as safe as your main computer. More about this in Chapter 11.

Finding Out More about Viruses

To look into the dark world of the viruses themselves, go to Chapters 13, 14, and 15. Here you can find out about the deranged people who write viruses and why they do it. I also explain more about how viruses and their cousins (worms and Trojan horses) cause damage and spread from computer to computer.

It makes sense (beyond my personal opinion) that knowing more about how viruses work will help you avoid them. The same goes for biological viruses: When you know how they spread, you can think before you act, and avoid them — maybe not every time, but much of the time. *Enough* of the time.

Chapter 3

Does Your Computer Have Antivirus Software?

....

In This Chapter

▶ Figuring out what antivirus software is

▶ Searching high and low for antivirus icons

▶ Asking the folks who sold you your computer

▶ Determining whether your antivirus software is working correctly

....

*T*o know whether your computer is protected against viruses and other threats, you need to know for certain whether you have antivirus software installed on your computer. That's because antivirus software is your best defense against viruses. Period.

Not only do you need to know whether you have antivirus software, but you need to know whether your antivirus software is actually working properly — which means (among other things) that it had better be up to date.

This chapter helps you figure out for sure whether or not you have antivirus software and whether it's functioning properly. This knowledge serves as a starting point toward identifying and getting rid of a virus that's already on your system and protecting your computer from future viruses.

Understanding Antivirus Software

Before I explain what antivirus software is, it's worth reviewing the nature of software in general. Understanding software doesn't mean you have to write computer programs or wear a hat with a propeller on top. The fact is that the word *software* is at the heart of viruses *and* the defenses against them. Knowing some basics about software will help you to understand viruses and how to stop them in their tracks.

These days, the term *software* is roughly synonymous with *computer program*. A *program* used to be a set of instructions individually written for every task a computer did. Software began as a package of programs designed to handle a range of specific tasks consistently. These days it's a packaged product that tells the computer what to do — consistently. There's the rub: A computer is, after all, a machine that's no smarter than its creators; software is still a set of instructions that makes the computer do everything. If a hacker can figure out *how* it does that, then the computer is ripe for a sneaky takeover.

Yep, viruses are software: Nasty, illicit software. As such, they can only be effectively fought with (you guessed it). . . .

Antivirus software is specifically designed to rid your computer of viruses and to keep them at bay, usually by three methods:

- ✔ By identifying viruses and arresting them when they try to invade
- ✔ By identifying viruses already present in the computer
- ✔ By removing viruses and making simple repairs to the computer

So your mission, should you choose to accept it, is to figure out whether you already have antivirus software on your computer and, if so, whether it's working.

Looking Around for Antivirus Icons

The first thing you can do to see if your computer has antivirus software is to look in a number of different places for specific icons that are associated with antivirus programs. Some of the places to look include the Start menu, your desktop, and your *system tray* (the area on the bottom right of your screen that contains, among other things, the time of day).

The presence of an antivirus icon on your Start menu or desktop is not proof positive that the associated antivirus program is actually on your computer. It's a pretty good indication, but not proof. To be completely literal, the presence of an antivirus icon on your Start menu means that *at one time* your computer had antivirus software; it *may* still have it, and it may not. (If your computer has an antivirus icon on the Start menu, but no antivirus software, then the antivirus software was probably removed, but the removal process forgot to remove the icon.)

If you find a familiar antivirus icon on your *system tray* (the area in the lower-right corner of your Windows screen, where the time is), it's a pretty good indication that your computer has antivirus software, and that it is running. It doesn't tell you about the *health* of your antivirus software, but at least you can know that it's there. You can double-click the icon and see whether anything shows up on-screen, but even that test won't tell you everything.

Time to discuss those indicators in detail.

Look in — or hunt for — the system tray

Check the system tray first, as this will give you an indication that you not only have antivirus software that is installed on your computer, but also that it is actually running.

The *system tray* (or, for the ultra-cyberhip, *systray*) is a part of your taskbar that contains several small icons — and usually also the time (sometimes the date).

The taskbar can be on the left side, right side, top, or bottom of your screen. If you don't see the taskbar, perhaps it has been set to Auto Hide (it becomes invisible unless the cursor is in the general area). Move your mouse to the top edge of the screen, then to the bottom edge, then left, then right. If your taskbar is set to Auto Hide, then moving the mouse to its hiding place causes the taskbar to appear.

Note the location of the system tray — it's at the opposite end of the taskbar from the Start button. If your taskbar also has a Quick Launch bar, it is usually right next to the Start button. (Have a look at Figure 3-1 to see what I'm talking about.)

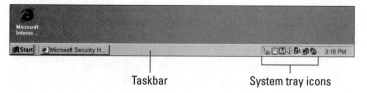

Taskbar   System tray icons

Figure 3-1: The taskbar, with the system tray and its icons.

Take a look in the system tray on your computer to see whether it holds one of the icons shown in Table 3-1.

 If your system tray icons seem too cryptic, cheat: Hover the mouse pointer over each one and look for a *tool tip* — a neat little label that identifies the program associated with the icon — to appear. For example, if you're running Norton AntiVirus and you hover the mouse pointer over the Norton AntiVirus system tray icon, you can see the text `Norton AntiVirus Auto-Protect Enabled` (if Norton AntiVirus is malfunctioning, it might say something else, such as `Norton AntiVirus Auto-Protect Disabled`).

Table 3-1	**Popular System Tray Icons**
Vendor	*Icons You'll See*
Trend PC-Cillin	
McAfee	

Vendor	Icons You'll See			
Symantec				
Panda				
CA eTrust				
Kaspersky				
NOD32				
Command				
Norman				
F-Secure				

If you don't find a system tray icon that's associated with an antivirus software program, that doesn't necessarily mean that you don't have antivirus software:

✔ Your antivirus program may have been manufactured before displaying a system tray icon became the norm. (Consider that a hint: An updated version would be a *really* good idea.)

✔ Your antivirus program may not be running now (that's a bad thing, by the way, because antivirus software should *always* be running).

✔ The built-in Windows feature called Windows Explorer (*not* the Web browser called Internet Explorer) may have been restarted on your computer; when this happens, some programs' system-tray icons disappear and don't come back until the system is rebooted (shame on any program that doesn't try to put its system-tray icon back!).

Look on the Start menu

If your antivirus program doesn't show up in the system tray, it may still be hanging around on your hard drive somewhere. Another reliable way to find out is to look at the Start menu. Figure 3-2 shows the Windows XP Start menu.

1. On the taskbar, click the Start button.

For those new to Windows, the Start button hangs out in the lower-left corner of the screen, at the left end of the taskbar. If the taskbar is playing hide-and-seek, bring it out of hiding (as noted in the "Look in — or hunt for — the system tray" section, earlier in this chapter). If you're running Windows XP, you then click All Programs unless you're using the "classic" Windows 2000 menu style.

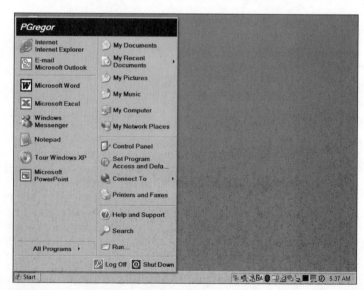

Figure 3-2: The Windows XP Start menu before clicking All Programs.

Your taskbar might not be on the bottom of the screen. You or someone else might have moved it to the top, right, or left side. Still, the taskbar will contain the Start button at one end and the system tray icons on the other end. And remember that the taskbar can be trained to hide itself, so you may need to start moving your mouse pointer to the top, left, and right edges to see if you can coax it out of hiding. If that doesn't work either, well, your computer might be really sick, old, or not running Windows!

2. **Find the antivirus program in the Start menu.**

   Depending on how it was installed (some programs have options that put Start menu items in unusual places), you may see the antivirus program manufacturer's name first; clicking on that gets you to another menu item, or possibly to the actual list of programs and features found in the antivirus program.

   Be patient. It can take quite a while to find your antivirus program's Start-menu entry, especially if you have a lot of software programs installed on your computer. The name might not be immediately obvious, either.

3. **If you find an antivirus program on the Start menu, start the program by clicking its entry in the menu.**

   If nothing appears to happen, consider:

   - You may have started the part of the antivirus program that runs in the background, watching for virus activities — in which case, you may not see any change in how your computer is running.

   - Are there any new icons in the system tray that you didn't see before? Often, when an antivirus program starts, even if it's running quietly in the background, it will place an icon in the system tray as a convenient way for you to find it and to get its status.

   - If you don't see any change and you find no new icons in the system tray, then you may have a problem with the antivirus program.

4. **If the antivirus program starts and you see some kind of a configuration window, I believe your search may be over.**

Oh, yeah, don't forget to give yourself a pat on the back. If it starts, you've found it. The next question is what to do with it. Proceed to Chapter 8 for instructions on updating your antivirus program's virus signatures — you need to do this prior to running a scan. Chapter 6 provides instructions on how to scan your computer for viruses.

If the antivirus program doesn't start, you can try a few other things:

✔ Try another item from the Start menu that you think may be a part of your antivirus software, especially if there was more than one icon associated with the antivirus program. Just don't select any "uninstall" item!

✔ If you see a Help item associated with your antivirus program, this might be helpful, as you may find specific instructions on how to start and manage your antivirus program.

✔ It's also possible that the antivirus software program was removed, but the removal process failed to get rid of the Start-menu items you found. If that's what happened, you see a window like the one in Figure 3-3.

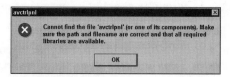

Figure 3-3: The Start menu cannot find the program associated with the icon.

Look on the desktop

Installation programs often place an icon on the desktop, so it's sensible to look on the desktop for an antivirus icon as a means of determining whether antivirus software is currently installed on your computer. This method is a little bit less reliable than searching the Start menu (as I describe in the previous section), for a couple of reasons:

✔ **Failing to find an icon on the desktop doesn't mean your computer lacks an antivirus program.** Perhaps when the antivirus program was installed, whoever installed it told the install program *not* to create desktop menu icons.

✔ **Finding an icon doesn't necessarily mean that the program is still present in your computer:** Sometimes "uninstall" programs fail to delete desktop icons.

That said, it's still worth taking a few minutes to look on the desktop for an antivirus icon. If your computer's icons are jumbled on top of each other, align them so you can see them all; if your computer has an antivirus program, the icon should turn up.

You can use a built-in Windows feature to align your icons instantly — just remember that you can't undo the command. If you want 'em back the way they were, you'll have to drag them to where you want them. Anyway, here's the drill:

✔ **Windows 2000:** Right-click the desktop and choose Line Up Icons.

✔ **Windows XP:** Right-click the desktop and choose Arrange Icons By➪Align to Grid.

If you did find icons on your desktop that are associated with an antivirus program, double-click 'em and see what happens. If you're lucky today, your computer *does* have antivirus software and you will see its main control panel program appear. (See Chapter 8 for how to update the antivirus program's virus signatures; Chapter 6 covers scanning for viruses.)

Look at installed programs

If you looked for desktop icons or Start menu items that may indicate an installed antivirus program (as I describe in the previous sections) and came up empty, you're not necessarily dead in the water. You can look at the list of installed programs to see whether antivirus software is installed. It's usually a reliable indicator.

This procedure consists of pulling up your computer's main control panel. There are a few different ways this is done, depending upon what operating system your computer is running and also how the control panel itself is configured. The basic scenario looks like this:

1. **Click the Start button on your Windows taskbar.**

   If you are running Windows 2000, you'll see a short menu appear.

2. **Choose Settings⇨Control Panel.**

   A new window opens or you see another set of choices appear in the Start menu.

3. **Choose Add/Remove Programs, as shown in Figure 3-4.**

   If you're running Windows XP, you might not see the Add/Remove Programs option in the control panel. If this is the case, find and click Switch to Classic View on the left side of the control panel. Then you can click Add/Remove Programs.

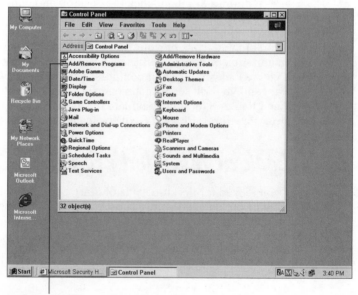

Click here to add or remove programs.

Figure 3-4: Windows 2000 control panel — "Classic View."

4. **With the Add/Remove Programs window open (as shown in Figure 3-5), examine this list for antivirus programs.**

Do not click any of these items; just scroll through the list. You cannot start your antivirus software program here — it's only the place where you would remove any installed software.

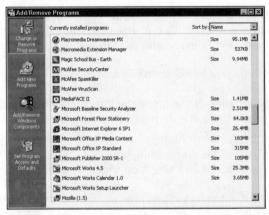

Figure 3-5: Windows 2000 — Add/Remove Programs window.

Asking at Your Place of Purchase

If you purchased your computer from a retailer, then you should examine all of the paperwork that came with your computer — perhaps something says which antivirus program was installed on your computer.

You could also visit the store where you purchased your computer and find someone who can help you. A salesperson, or someone in the service department, should be able to help you. This depends, though, on how long ago you purchased your computer — the people in the store may not remember what antivirus software (if any) was installed on computers in the distant past.

Checking the Health of Your Antivirus Software

After you locate the antivirus software on your computer, you need to "look under the hood" and see whether it appears to be operating properly.

Until you are more familiar with your computer and its antivirus software, it's not wise to assume that your antivirus software is configured and operating correctly.

The steps you follow here will accomplish two things:

- ✔ You will be confirming the important aspects of your antivirus software in order to determine if it's working right.

- ✔ You will be discovering how your antivirus software is configured and how it operates on your computer.

The next sections explain how to make your antivirus software open up and say, "Aaaaah."

Step 1: Determining whether your antivirus software starts at bootup

When you start ("boot") the computer, the computer's startup instructions direct several features and programs to begin running. Here are some ways to figure out if antivirus software begins to run on your computer:

- ✔ **Check for a splash screen:** When some of these programs start, they display a *splash screen* on the computer's monitor. A splash screen is sort of like a ten-second "look at me, I'm starting!" advertisement. Most, if not all, antivirus tools display some sort of a splash screen when they start. I have included some antivirus program splash screens in Figure 3-6.

Figure 3-6: Some antivirus program splash screens.

The absence of a splash screen does not conclusively prove the absence of an antivirus program. Some antivirus programs do not have splash screens; also, some programs let you exclude the splash screen display. That said, if you see an antivirus splash screen, it's a pretty good indicator that your computer has an antivirus program that starts when the computer is started.

✓ **Look for system-tray icons:** The next thing to look for when checking the health of your antivirus software is to look for its system tray icon. The presence of a system tray icon is a pretty good indicator that the antivirus program not only started, but has managed to keep running. You're not out of the woods yet, though.

✓ **Can you see the status:** Now you need to see if you can coax the antivirus program to show you a detailed status and configuration screen. How to do this will vary somewhat depending on which antivirus software program is running on your computer. Here are a few things you can try:

  • **Click the antivirus system-tray icon.** If a menu appears, see what options are available. Items like Options, Configure, and Status sound like good things to try. An About item would also be good, as you'll get to see the full name and version of your antivirus program.

- **Double-click the system tray icon.** This may cause a configuration program or status program to appear — again, this depends upon the brand of antivirus program you're using. They all run a little bit differently.

  - **Right-click the system-tray icon.** As with the single-click above, this could get you a menu with some options to try.

If none of these does anything, then you'll have to start the antivirus program's configuration screen some other way. For other possible ways of starting antivirus software, use the methods that I describe earlier in the "Look on the Start menu" and "Look on the desktop" sections.

Assuming that one of the things here got your antivirus program going and displaying some sort of a status or configuration screen, there are some things to look for in the upcoming sections.

Step 2: Determining the version of antivirus software

On the splash screen, system tray icon, or desktop icon — or on the program's status screen — you should see the brand name of the antivirus software. Or you can start the antivirus program and choose Help➪About. You want to get the version name and number of the software too.

There are a couple of reasons to do this. If you know what make and version of antivirus software you have, you can visit the software maker's Web site and get more information about the product: You can find help in the form of support information, frequently-asked questions, and how-to instructions for operating the program.

Also, in general, you can find answers to other questions when you know what make and version your antivirus software is. For instance, you may need to find out how to configure another program if part of that program's configuration depends on which antivirus program you're using.

Step 3: Figuring out when the last update occurred

The most important thing to figure out when you're working with existing antivirus software is when the program's virus definitions were last updated. Depending on which antivirus program you have, this might be displayed on the configuration screen. If not, it could be in Help⇨About, or in the About option from the system tray. Every antivirus program displays this information a little differently. You gotta love the consistency between the different antivirus programs.

If the date of the last update is within the past couple of weeks, then you can be pretty sure that your antivirus software is working okay, at least up to that date. Also, provided that your antivirus software is configured properly, you'll be protected against all but the very latest viruses.

If, on the other hand, the date of the last update is older than a few weeks, then you need to update your virus-definition files as soon as possible. You can find detailed information on how to do this in Chapter 8.

Many antivirus programs will give you the dates of your most recent last update, last scan, and program version if you choose Help⇨About.

Step 4: Figuring out when the last scan occurred

While you're checking out your antivirus program, you also need to figure out when your computer was last scanned for viruses.

Like the date of the last virus-definitions file, the date of the last virus scan is important to know. However, the last scan date is not quite as important as the date of the virus-definition file update.

If the date of the last virus definition update *and* the date of the last scan are both more than a few weeks in the past, you may be several thousand viruses behind the times (this should not make you feel old). Update your virus definitions first, and then scan the computer for viruses.

Part II
Deploying Your Antivirus Defenses

The 5th Wave   By Rich Tennant

HELP DESK

TECHNICAL   ETHICAL

In this part . . .

So you're in the market for antivirus software? You need to stick with known name brand antivirus programs and buy one from a trustworthy source. Should you buy a CD-ROM or a download version? (Personally, I would go with the CD version.) When you install your antivirus software, I strongly recommend that you perform a full computer scan if the installation procedure provides for it.

After your antivirus software is installed, it's time to set up regular scans and signature file updates. How often should these be done? It depends partly on how you use the computer. If your antivirus program provides specialized e-mail protection, you want to set this up as well. Likewise, if you use instant messaging and your antivirus program can protect it, then by all means you need to enable this too.

Scanning your computer for viruses is a basic task that you need to be familiar with. You want to configure your antivirus program to do scans in the middle of the night, or whenever you aren't using your computer for a while. You also want to know how to start a scan of a file, directory, or the entire computer if you suspect that a virus may be in your computer.

If your computer has a virus, you've got to get rid of it as quickly and carefully as possible. Your antivirus software can remove many viruses, but some require specialized tools that are usually available from antivirus companies. But sometimes, the damage from a virus can be so devastating that you need to reinstall Windows. Yuck.

Chapter 4

Obtaining and Installing Antivirus Software

● ●

In This Chapter

▶ Choosing brand-name antivirus software

▶ Making an informed decision about antivirus software

▶ Kicking your current antivirus program to the curb (or just upgrading it)

▶ Purchasing antivirus software: How and where

▶ Getting through the installation (sheesh!)

● ●

This chapter is intended to make you a good, informed shopper. Stick with me and you'll know just what you're looking for. I describe many of the features that can be found on antivirus programs — one or more of these features may well be something you want.

I also help you install your antivirus software. Each of them is a little different, but the concepts are pretty much the same on all of the antivirus programs.

Sticking with Name Brands You Know

If you're going to take any of my advice seriously, put this bit at the top of the list: It's vitally important that you use known and reputable antivirus software.

Does it really matter which *brand* of antivirus software you purchase?

If you buy any of the top ten or so brands of consumer antivirus software, and if you properly configure and operate the program, you have good protection against viruses. So, *no,* it doesn't matter which *brand* you select. What is far more important is that you purchase antivirus software that meets two criteria:

✔ It includes the features you need.

✔ It's easy for you to use.

On the first point about features, you'll discover more about features as you read this book. Most antivirus products are fully functional by themselves, but many are now "bundled" with other products such as antispam software, firewalls, pop-up blockers, and plastic toy handcuffs for when you catch a hacker yourself.

I cannot express enough that whichever product you select should be easy for you to use. If the product you choose is difficult for you to understand or operate, you might not understand what is going on and you could possibly misconfigure it. Or, worse, you might give up altogether, leaving you vulnerable to new viruses and worms.

This isn't too much different from VCR's. If you can't quite figure out how to program your VCR, you might miss your favorite episode of Iron Chef or Jerry Springer (I'm trying to appeal to both ends of the spectrum here). The consequences of your failing to properly program your VCR may be that you miss your favorite TV show, whereas the consequences of failing to configure your antivirus program could result in a virus getting into your computer, stealing your credit-card numbers and buying phone calling cards or VCRs from cheezy online merchants. Or worse.

When you are buying antivirus software, you are not just purchasing a tool — you are entering into a long-term relationship. When you choose a particular brand of antivirus software, you are immediately becoming dependent upon the quality of that company's product — including the competence of their antivirus research labs and their capability to develop and send you the data that your antivirus software needs to stop the very latest viruses, worms, and Trojan horses.

If you're going to skimp, then do so elsewhere: buy cheap speakers, or a crummy mouse, or a monitor that is too small, dim, or wavy. None of these will endanger your information — or make your life as miserable as a substandard antivirus program can.

A good antivirus software program is worth far more than the price you pay for it, *the very first time* it stops a virus. And these days, that could be the very day you first install it! Chapter 17 provides a group of antivirus programs that you can count on along with Web sites for more information.

Considering Important Antivirus Features

You need to be a good consumer — a smart shopper. If you really don't have a clue about what you need in an antivirus program, then the also-clueless salesperson at your favorite computer store could steer you toward something that may not meet your needs.

Of course, if the store salesman turns out not to know much, you can (and should) find another salesman or another store. But another really great thing you can do is compare product features online. Virtually all decent antivirus products (even some of the indecent ones) have Web sites that describe features and functions in detail, sometimes including screen shots.

Fee or free subscription?

A vital part of an antivirus program is the capability to download new virus-definition files from the software vendor. Without this feature, your antivirus program won't be worth much at all — the newest viruses are often the ones that get you. If your antivirus product isn't downloading new virus-definition files, then you're not protected against the viruses likeliest to do you harm. Bad.

Virtually all antivirus products have a download feature, so what's the point? It's this: Many vendors let you download their virus definitions for a limited period of time (usually one year), after which you must renew your "subscription" if you want to keep downloading new virus definitions (you do!).

Other antivirus products do not charge for the right to download, but let you do so for free, for as long as you use the product. However, sooner or later you'll want to upgrade the product itself, so you'll have to pony up for the software upgrade. Those are *never* free! Regardless of how they get your money in exchange for the service they provide, they get your money. I think it's a fair deal. 'Nuff said.

Many computers now come with an antivirus program already installed — and usually that antivirus program provides full protection against viruses — but in many cases, the "subscription" is for a short period of time, perhaps just 90 days. That's just enough time for you to get used to (and, so the makers hope, fall in love with) their product, so you won't hesitate to purchase a full one-year subscription.

So it's true that the antivirus vendors want to get on the gravy train and make money. Ain't capitalism great?!

My final thought on this: You get what you pay for. I personally would stay away from a no-name free or nearly-free antivirus program, and instead stick with the major brand of antivirus software that I use. Cheap antivirus software is like cheap tires: How much risk are you willing to accept?

Scanning: Manual and scheduled

You should be able to manually and easily scan individual files, directories, or your entire computer. An especially nice feature is the ability to scan right from your Windows Explorer program by right-clicking a file or directory and selecting the Scan for Viruses feature.

Likewise, scheduling scans should also be easy to figure out, and these days it had *better* be easier than programming a VCR — even the fancy on-screen-programming models. Just make sure you can schedule scans to take place daily, weekly, or at whatever schedule is appropriate for you.

Compatibility with your e-mail program

Even the best antivirus program can't do its job unless it can play nice with your e-mail program. Two types of e-mail programs are the most common:

> ✔ **Local e-mail clients:** If you use a local e-mail client program (such as Outlook, Outlook Express, or Eudora) that connects directly to your Internet service provider, check to make sure the antivirus program you choose is compatible with the specific e-mail program you're using.

> ✔ **Web e-mail clients:** If you use your Web browser to read and send e-mail, then compatibility with an antivirus program is not so much of an issue. This is because e-mail messages sent to you are not stored on your computer; instead, they're stored on your mail-service provider's Web server. All the antivirus programs that employ "real-time" virus detection protect you against viruses that try to come through Web e-mail clients. This is because viruses are stored in e-mail attachments — if you try to download a virus-borne attachment, your antivirus program will intercept it when your computer tries to store the attachment on your hard drive.

Virus-definition updates

Virus-definition updates are like your antivirus program's "air supply" — it can't function well without them. If any feature of your antivirus program absolutely *must* be flexible and easy to use, it's this function.

If you have a high-speed connection and valuable information on your computer to protect, then you need to automatically update your antivirus definitions frequently. If you choose to do so every hour, or twice a day, or at any time of day or night, your software should be able to do so easily.

If your needs are more modest — especially if you usually access the Internet using dial-up — then your antivirus software should be able to coax your computer into initiating a dial-up Internet connection as part of the downloading process. This capability will also depend on how your computer's Internet connection is configured.

Fix and recovery

It's nice when an antivirus program is able to detect a virus, but more important still is, what will the antivirus program *do* about it?

Will it say, "Hey bub, I see a virus there, good luck!"?

Or will it tell you, "Say, I see a virus here, and if you'd like to fix it, you'll need to visit our Web site for instructions on how to surgically remove it from your computer"? Nice. (Gee, thanks.)

Or, will your antivirus program say, "There *was* a virus there, and I've removed it"? That's my preference — how about you?

Special removal tools

I should say this: It's one thing to destroy viruses, worms, and Trojan horses when they're *attempting* to infiltrate your computer, but quite another if a virus has *already* penetrated your computer. In particular, when a worm has installed itself on a computer (because the computer's antivirus signatures weren't up to date), the antivirus program does not block the virus because it doesn't recognize it as such.

In this case, bringing the antivirus signature files up to date, and even rescanning the computer to remove any viruses, may not necessarily be enough to completely eradicate the virus. This may be true if the virus has employed unusual methods of installing itself. But the antivirus vendors have an answer for this.

Antivirus software vendors build specialized removal tools that are custom-tailored to remove every last trace of a virus that has dug its way into your computer's inner workings.

I suggest that you explore the Web sites of one or more vendors whose antivirus software programs you're considering. Check out their specialized removal tools. If there happens to be a severe outbreak when you read this, it will probably not be difficult to find removal tools for the current worm or virus. As it happens, though, old viruses never die, so the antivirus companies tend to keep all their old virus-removal tools on the Web site as well.

Other antivirus makers may have what you need

Outside of their apparent fondness for Microsoft applications, viruses have no brand loyalty. Whichever brand of antivirus software you eventually choose, you don't have to stick with the special virus removal tools offered by your brand. Another company may offer an effective tool that you can use right away. For instance, you might use McAfee antivirus software, but you could easily download a virus-removal tool from Symantec, Trend Micro, or Computer Associates.

Bundling other features

Market forces have compelled antivirus software makers to bundle other products or features with their programs. For instance, many antivirus programs include a firewall, spam blocker, or pop-up blocker. They're worth taking a look at in terms of the additional protection they offer.

Blocking worms and scans with a firewall

Firewall programs have become quite popular, and for good reason: Many of the threats present today aren't totally addressed by antivirus programs.

A lot of hackers *scan* networks (scanning means that they send thousands or even millions of network probes through the Internet) in search of computers that have been configured incorrectly. Such misconfigurations enable the hackers to exploit security flaws and do these typical dirty deeds:

 ✔ Installing backdoor programs and using your computer (and hundreds or thousands of others) to relay spam messages all over the Web. Read the sidebar "The Legion of Zombies" in Chapter 1 to see what a back door is.

✔ Using your computer to bomb some Web site in a Distributed Denial of Service (DDoS) attack. The sidebar "The legion of zombies" in Chapter 1 provides more information on DDoS attacks.

✔ Searching your computer for sensitive personal information such as credit-card, bank-account, or tax-ID numbers.

Internet worms are also a threat, although not as serious a threat as hackers themselves because an up-to-date antivirus program will prevent a worm from installing itself on your computer. Still, having a firewall provides some *defense in depth* (you know, like adding an alarm system behind your moat) by blocking the scanning probes sent by hackers and Internet worms. Worms are described in detail in Chapter 14.

Slaying spam

If you *like* getting dozens of unsolicited e-mail messages every day, you can skip this section.

Everybody still with me? Thought so. If you are using a local e-mail client such as Outlook Express or Eudora, then antispam software can considerably reduce the amount of unwanted e-mail.

If you use Web-based e-mail, chances are your e-mail provider (at least the larger ones) is using spam blocking — it might not be free, though. Something about profit motive comes to mind.

Antispam software accomplishes this improvement in two primary ways:

✔ **By keyword:** The software searches for keywords and key phrases in all messages; any messages that match the keywords are blocked.

✔ **By whitelisting:** That's the opposite of blacklisting. Any message that comes from someone on your list of known senders (your whitelist) is permitted; all others are blocked. Simple, huh?

I have some opinions about spam-blocking programs — and most industry analysts agree with me (or I with them):

Although it's a great idea, spam-blocking software is far from perfect. This is because the people who write spam try very hard to build messages that don't get blocked. It's a classic good guys-versus-bad-guys situation online — the good guys fight the bad guys and their hats don't even fall off! Go rent an old John Wayne movie sometime and you'll see what I'm talking about.

Flattening pop-ups

Certainly you've been to one of those Web sites that plasters those annoying pop-up ads all over your screen, trying to sell you life insurance, travel helps, online dating, sex toys, or (yeah, right) pop-up blockers. Well, maybe the sex toys are okay, especially the *<censored by editor>*. Oops. (Just kidding.)

You can do away with those annoying pop-up ads with a special pop-up blocking tool, included with some antivirus programs. Norton AntiVirus and Trend Micro's PC-Cillin have available pop-up blockers — but blocking pop-ups is likely to be included with most antivirus programs before too long.

Neutering spyware

Spyware is a new class of software used to track what you're doing on your computer so other people (or companies) can study how you use it.

If you are not concerned about this potential invasion of privacy, I think you should be — but that's just my opinion, my unsolicited advice. I'm not about to panic over someone tracking my Internet-surfing habits, any more than I am about large grocery-store chains knowing my grocery-purchasing habits. But others of you may be concerned — perhaps furious — about this. If you are concerned about online privacy and spyware, then you should consider getting a spyware blocker.

You can still find some of the better antispyware available as separate programs, but I suspect that the smaller of those software companies are going to be snatched up by the big antivirus vendors in order to get those cool spyware blockers bundled with antivirus programs.

You're probably wondering where to find some of these anti-spyware programs. I'll describe some of my favorites here:

- ✔ **Ad-Aware:** This is one of the pioneers, and they keep making it better.

- ✔ **Spybot:** Another nice one. It blocks ActiveX and JavaScript controls, and lets you protect some IE browser settings too. It has nice features for advanced users too.

- ✔ **Spyware Blaster:** A "preventive" antispyware program that prevents spyware from getting into your computer in the first place.

You can find all of these at download.com, one of my favorite places for finding new goodies. Do be careful, though, not to bloat your computer with too many bells and whistles!

You can also find more ideas for antispyware on my Web site, www.computervirusesbook.com. (Sorry, long name — you'd better bookmark it.)

Upgrading and Switching Brands

The online environment of the Internet continues to mutate (as do the hackers); users must change their defensive tactics or suffer (at least) trashed hard drives and lost data. Hype aside, no one company is likely to have all the answers to all possible threats for all time. Sooner or later, you pretty much have to face upgrading your antivirus software — or even changing vendors.

Reasons to upgrade

Perhaps you already have an antivirus program on your computer, and you are considering upgrading to a newer version of the program. There are several reasons why you might wish to upgrade, including:

- ✔ **The version you have is so *old* that you can no longer get virus definitions for it.** For a variety of reasons, antivirus software makers stop producing updates for older versions of their software. This is partly because those older versions just don't have some of the capabilities that the newer ones have.

✔ **The newer version may be *easier to use* than the version you have today.** It is true that "user interfaces" (the windows, buttons, tabs, and so on that you see when operating a program) have generally improved on many products over the years as software producers have slowly begun to figure out how to make easy-to-use software. If your software is more than three years old, then this may be reason enough!

✔ **The newer version may have *more features*.** The antivirus software market is becoming increasingly competitive, prompting the antivirus software companies to keep up with one another. Prices haven't been dropping, but instead they keep packing in more features and functions — another benefit of this competition.

✔ **The newer version may *work better* with your computer's operating system or e-mail program.** No contest there.

✔ **Your *expert friend* says it's a good idea.** Well, if your friend is *really* an expert and not just someone who *wants* to be, then this can truly be a legitimate reason to upgrade. Either way, ask him or her the *reason* for the upgrade. Does the explanation make sense to you?

✔ **You love to buy and install software because *it's fun*.** Tell you what: As a gesture of goodwill toward the exotic planet you must come from, I could ask you over to install a few fancy programs on *my* computer, but let's get yours done first.

Now, I'm not going to tell you that any of these reasons — or any others — are enough by themselves to make you consider upgrading your antivirus software. In the end, it's up to you. Think about your current situation and the desired outcome. Can you get there from here?

Reasons to switch brands

You traitor, you! Seriously, though, there are a number of valid reasons why you may be considering changing brands of antivirus software. I'll go over a few here:

✓ **You want to change to a *well-known* brand.** I can't blame you if you feel like you're "missing the boat" by sticking with Bill and Ted's Most Excellent Antivirus program. This is a truly legitimate reason to change. The virus threat is getting more complicated, requiring a larger research-and-development budget from all antivirus software companies. The smaller companies are not going to be able to keep up with the giants.

✓ **You want a more *reputable* brand of antivirus software.** If the brand you are using now is associated with some kind of colossal error, you may be compelled to switch. Well, it's important that you use a brand that you can trust. I can't offer any hints here — truly I cannot recall any gaffes perpetrated by any of the major brands. Little mistakes — sure — but nothing approaching scandal material.

✓ ***Other computers* in your home or business are using another brand.** Fer shure, it's easier to do the antivirus thang if all of the computers are running the same program. There is less you have to remember, and it's probably more economical to buy 5-license, 10-license, or 25-license packages instead of a lot of single-user licenses. Consistency is a good thing.

✓ **The brand you want has *better features* or is *easier to use*.** The hassle factor alone can be reason enough.

✓ **Your old brand *isn't working*.** I have switched brands of antivirus software in the past. The old brand was wasting my time and making me angry, and their tech support was next to worthless. So I switched. 'Nuf said!

✓ **Your *expert friend* is more familiar with a different brand.** A lot can be said about expert friends, especially when they are *real* experts and when they are *really* willing to help you. If this is the case, you might be better off switching to the one they know. (A real expert can spell *heuristics* backwards and explain it to you.)

Oftentimes, switching brands has as much to do with emotion as it does with performance or compatibility (except for compatibility with *you*). That's okay — if there's any software you need to be comfortable with, it's your antivirus software. It's a lot like automobile tires or insurance: Reliability and performance are *not* optional.

Upgrading or switching brands safely

Upgrading safely? Switching brands safely? Is there potential danger involved with upgrading or switching brands of antivirus software? Well, yes, there can be. But that's no reason to shy away from the task — you just can't pretend it's a non-issue, either. Here's what's going on. . . .

You need to understand the steps involved in the operation of switching or upgrading (whichever is the case for you). Primarily, the reason for this is that there may be a period of time during which your old antivirus software isn't running and the new antivirus software isn't yet fully functional.

Here's how the gap in protection can take place. You may need to remove your old antivirus program before upgrading or installing the new one. When you remove your old antivirus program, you are temporarily going without that protection on your computer, until you have installed and configured the new antivirus program.

Here are some guidelines to consider when upgrading or switching brands:

1. **Read the instructions for both your old antivirus and the new antivirus program before you begin.**

2. **Keep the old virus software running, if possible.**

3. **Back up your critical data files.**

   I talk your ear off about backups in Chapter 12.

4. **Disconnect from the Internet if you are able to do so during the installation or upgrade; stay that way until you're sure the new antivirus software is working properly.**

5. **Close all other programs during the install or upgrade until you are sure that the new antivirus program is working.**

6. **Install critical security patches before you begin.**

   I discuss this topic in detail in Chapter 9.

If you do install one or more patches, I advise you to run your computer for at least several hours, if not a day or two, before also changing out your antivirus software.

7. **Reboot *before* you begin the removal or upgrade process.**

Start with a clean-running system! This is especially important on the older versions of Windows that — rumor has it — are equipped with the fabled "time to crash!" feature.

Checking Out the Purchasing Venues

It's time to do some serious window shopping. I don't know if you have chosen a brand and model of antivirus software, or if you'll "kick the tires" while looking around in order to make your final decision.

Personally, I don't like making impulsive decisions when making a major purchase (and, despite the relatively low price tag for antivirus software, I consider it a "major purchase" because of its relatively *high importance*). Buying antivirus software is like buying insurance: It's important to make a good choice now *just in case* you need the assistance later. Remember, however, that with antivirus software, you need that assistance every day!

Depending upon where you live, you might have good access to one or more large computer stores; otherwise, you might have to do your shopping and comparing online.

I do suggest that you do some online shopping; you can find out a lot about what's available by comparing products online. This is because many computer stores — even the larger ones — usually carry only two or three brands of antivirus software — possibly your first or second choice won't even be available locally. (For more about buying online, see the upcoming — you guessed it — "Buying online" section.)

Buying at computer stores

Personally I like to do hands-on shopping. Picking up the package, talking to real salespeople, and readily seeing prices has a lot of value for me (okay, call me old-fashioned). Computer stores usually have demo computers, perhaps with one or more of the brands of antivirus software that you can look at, test drive, and ask questions about.

But the downside of shopping in computer stores is often the limited selection and the difficulty of doing a thorough comparison between brands. But you *can* walk out of the store with an antivirus program, very likely a reputable brand.

If you're buying a computer from the computer store, you need to know which antivirus software is included with the computer. Ask these questions (and perhaps more):

- ✔ **What brand and version of antivirus software is included with the computer?**

- ✔ **Is the antivirus software preinstalled, or must I install it myself?** If you are unfamiliar with how to install the software, perhaps the store will install it for you, if that will make you feel better.

- ✔ **Is the antivirus software fully functional as is, or is it a limited-function "demo" package?** Bottom line, demos mean you're under a deadline to shell out more for the full version before the demo period runs out.

- ✔ **For what period of time am I entitled to get virus-definition updates?** Often, the antivirus software bundled with a new computer has a limited-time subscription, perhaps just 30 or 60 days. Other bundle deals are more generous and will give you a full year.

Buying online

When choosing a reputable merchant, purchasing antivirus software online can be a rewarding experience. And if you're into instant gratification — or at least instant spending without leaving the house — then online shopping is for you.

Can you download it again?

If you purchase the download version of antivirus software (or, indeed, any other software), you'll either be down-loading the full product or a small installer program. If you get the full product, you could always burn it onto a CD-ROM in case you need to install it again, say, after you upgrade your operating system or you upgrade your computer.

But if you need to reinstall your antivirus software, will its maker *permit* you to download it again? Honestly, I haven't checked this out with every antivirus company, but I've seen it both ways: one company wants to charge you $6.95 for what they call "download service" — the right to download the product *again* if you have to — and another company lets you download the product for free, as many times as necessary.

Those companies that charge this fee are not going to tell you this up-front, however. They wait until you're in the checkout line and you're already writing the check. By then they've got you! Perhaps the best way to find this out is to load up the download version into your online shopping cart, and pay attention as you get into the checkout line. If you see an offer that permits unlimited downloads for a fee, then you need to figure that into the total cost.

Only buy from the maker's official site

Some may argue this point, but it's hard to go wrong if you purchase your antivirus software from the maker's own Web site. You're sure to get *the very latest* software from its source.

 Before deciding to buy from a reseller rather than the official maker, make sure you will be able to get help if you need it. Find out where you will be able to get that help. But the time to investigate this may not be worth the modest savings you realize.

Do NOT buy from a spammer

I'm a principled individual. I happen to detest spam (in fact, I'm not sure I know *anyone* who *likes* it), and because of that I refuse to purchase anything from a spammer, and I refuse to even visit their Web sites. The more that people ignore spam, the sooner many of the spam operators will go and find a more reputable line of work (like telemarketing or used car sales) and leave your inbox alone.

Direct download or CD?

When purchasing antivirus software (and most other software) online, you often have the choice of directly downloading the software, or you can purchase a CD to be shipped to you. Often there's a discount for purchasing the download, because you're saving the software vendor a few dollars (and *only* a few dollars).

But let me tell you my personal preference: Buy the CD. There are several good reasons why you would want to do so:

- ✔ If your computer crashes, you won't have to re-download your antivirus software. Instead, you can load it directly from the CD.

- ✔ If you upgrade your computer, you can just reinstall your antivirus software from the CD, which will probably be faster than downloading it again.

- ✔ If you must remove and reinstall your antivirus software, you wouldn't necessarily want to keep your computer online without virus protection during the entire download procedure.

- ✔ Some antivirus companies use a *bootable CD* that can be used to boot up, scan, and clean your system should you have a particularly nasty virus that can't be fixed by any other means. I find this more elegant and effective than creating a boot disk.

Installing Antivirus Software

This is the "let's do it!" part of the chapter where you get to actually *do something*. For those of you who are squirming at the chance to install software, you're almost there!

Do yourself a favor, though. Read *and follow* the checklist below before you begin installing your antivirus software.

If you're like me and you want to begin building the ready-to-assemble furniture or child's bicycle *before* reading the instructions, be prepared to have minutes — or hours — of regret later. I'm not kidding. The regret I speak of could be as minor as some lost time, or as great as losing files you cannot afford to be without. This is especially true if you make your living with your computer — whether you peddle prescription drugs online, sell things on eBay, or write books.

Here's what to do before installing your antivirus software:

- ✔ **Back up your files:** I don't mean copy them to another directory on the same hard drive — that would be like making copies of important documents and putting them in the same drawer. Convenient — until you have a fire. Instead, copy everything to another computer, or to a CD-ROM *that you have verified is readable on another computer.* Chapter 12 discusses backups in more detail.

- ✔ **Reboot your system:** 'Tis better to have a clean-running system that's not teetering on the edge of a crash because too many days have passed since the last reboot. (That's especially a problem on older Windows systems such as Windows 95, Windows 98, or Windows ME.)

- ✔ **Stop all of your other programs:** This includes all of the clutter in your systray, half of which you probably don't need or use anyway.

- ✔ **Read *all the way* through the antivirus program installation and/or upgrade instructions:** Wouldn't you just hate yourself if Step 46 said to do something that's really hard to do without a specific preparation that's only mentioned in Step 46? (I'm not much of a cook, and many times I've regretted not reading the recipe *all the way through* before starting, only to find that I lacked some important ingredient or didn't have enough time to prepare.)

- ✔ **Take notes:** Write down some of the essential things along the way — you may wish you had those little tidbits of data later. A few examples include the name of the directory where you installed the software, and the installation options that you chose.

- ✔ **Take your time:** If you hurry, you're more likely to skip an important step or make a mistake. It's more important to install your antivirus software *correctly* than quickly. You have to live with the results, probably for a long time. Quality doesn't take shortcuts, and neither should you.

> ✔ **Consider getting help:** If installing software feels as
> intimidating as rebuilding an automobile engine or pro-
> gramming a VCR, then consider having a PC expert help
> you out, or at least watch over your shoulder and tact-
> fully refrain from snickering to him- or herself.

Following a typical installation sequence

I'll skip the open-the-package and save-everything-in-it steps. I
figure you know how to do these things already. The following
sections provide step-by-step instructions on the process of
actually installing (what a concept) your antivirus software.

Step 1: Remove old antivirus software

Am I contradicting myself? Earlier in this chapter I tell you
to keep your old antivirus software running while you install
your new software. Although this is generally right, it may be
terribly wrong. There are two possibilities (and the only way
to figure out which is right is to read the documentation with
your antivirus software):

> ✔ **The software vendor wants you to keep your old version
> running.** This is more likely the case if you're staying with
> the same *brand* of antivirus software and just upgrading
> (the installation sequence for the new program may
> remove the old version automatically and even import
> your old settings).

> ✔ **The software vendor wants you to uninstall your old
> antivirus software.** Some antivirus programs fight each
> other to the death, like two capons (male chickens, for
> lack of a better word that the FCC won't fine me for) in
> the same pen, if you try to install one while the other is
> running. And, as an added bonus, *you* get to clean up the
> aftermath.

If you need to remove your old antivirus software, follow
these steps:

1. **Open the Windows control panel by choosing Start⇨
   Settings⇨Control Panel.**

2. **Select Add/Remove Programs.**

3. **Find your old antivirus program on the list, click it, and answer the questions to remove the software.**

   It's possible that there is more than one entry associated with your old antivirus program, so you'll need to go back and get them all. See Figure 4-1 for an example of the box that appears when you've found one to uninstall.

Figure 4-1: Removing your old antivirus software.

Step 2: Run the installation program

If you downloaded your new antivirus software from the vendor's Web site, go ahead and run that installation program now. If you are installing from a CD, insert the CD and follow the installation instructions (which may include booting your computer from the CD and performing some preliminary scans).

You will probably have several decisions to make, such as these:

- ✔ **The directory where the software should be installed:** Just go with the default.

- ✔ **Whether it should perform a complete virus scan of your computer:** Be patient and let it go through this process.

- ✔ **Whether you want the program to install a system tray icon:** Hint: You do!

- ✔ **Whether the antivirus program should start when the computer reboots:** Yes, yes, yes!

- ✔ **Whether the antivirus program should check removable media (floppy, CD, and so on) before the computer is shut down.** Yes, to prevent booting your computer from a virus-infected floppy or CD.

- ✔ **Whether the antivirus program should monitor all computer hard drive operations to check for viruses as they try to install themselves.** Yes, do this.

> ✔ **Whether the antivirus program should look for viruses in** *some* **types of files, or in** *all* **types of files.** I vote for *all types of files.* This is *not* a corner for cutting.

> ✔ **Whether the antivirus program should regularly scan your entire computer for viruses.** Most definitely yes!

Step 3: Connect to the Internet

The new antivirus software is going to need to download the very latest virus definitions. The definitions on the CD or download are likely to be at least several weeks or months old, which is an eternity in Internet time.

You may have to tell your antivirus program how to connect to the Internet. Some antivirus programs are smart enough to figure this out; others are as dumb as a post and need to be told every little detail:

> ✔ **If you have a cable modem, DSL, or some other "always on" Internet connection, then you will need to choose the "Direct Connection" option:** The option may be worded differently — software vendors usually try to be original, so there are different words and phrases that describe the same thing. Have a look at Figure 4-2.

> ✔ **If you dial up to the Internet using ISDN or your phone line, then you will need to tell your antivirus program how this is done:** The smarter antivirus programs will automatically delve into your computer's network connection configuration and figure this out for you; others are not so smart and will need to be spoon-fed.

To find your network configuration settings, go into your Network Connections configuration (Start⇨Settings⇨ Control Panel⇨Network Connections). See how your computer connects to the Internet (such as a dial-up connection, a LAN connection, and so on). Go back to the Internet Properties (refer to Figure 4-2) and see what "dialer" is used to connect to the Internet. The dialers are the items in the window right below Dial-up and Virtual Private Network Settings.

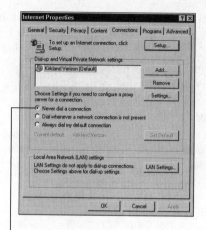

Typical setting for "always-on" connections.

Figure 4-2: Internet properties.

Step 4: Scan your computer for viruses

After getting the latest virus definitions, your new antivirus program will want to scan your entire computer for viruses. Do not skip this step. If your computer had been limping along on nonexistent, poorly functioning, or out-of-date antivirus software, there's a real chance that a virus got in. Get rid of it as soon as possible.

Step 5: Reboot your computer

Chances are the antivirus installation sequence will require one or more reboots. Pay attention to whether it asks you to remove the CD before rebooting (if you installed from a CD).

Creating rescue disks

Installation is not complete until you have made your rescue disk(s).

What's a rescue disk for? Generally, if you're unable to boot your computer because of a virus, a Rescue Disk just might save your day — it can get your computer running so you can do battle with the intruder. Go to Chapter 7 to read about using a Rescue Disk.

Open your antivirus program and look for the "Create a Rescue Disk" feature — most antivirus programs have this. If yours has this, go ahead and do it now: After all the time you've spent researching, buying, and installing, creating a Rescue Disk is probably the best five minutes you'll spend. Figure 4-3 shows a Rescue Disk in mid-creation with McAfee VirusScan.

You'll need a floppy disk. After you create the rescue disk, be sure to write-protect it, label it, and keep it in a safe place!

Figure 4-3: Creating a Rescue Disk.

Chapter 5

Configuring Antivirus Software

*G*oing to the trouble to properly configure your antivirus software can make your life easier down the road. Isn't it easier — and less stressful — to set up your antivirus software to update its database of computer viruses automatically at night, as you dream of relaxing on the beach of a tropical paradise, than to have to put your latest deadline on hold because a killer worm is ravaging computers across the world and you haven't updated your antivirus signatures in a month?

Antivirus software programs have a multitude of settings, configurations, check boxes, and other gizmos that, although appearing complicated at first, are really simple after you understand what they're for and how they work. This chapter is where you get to sit at the controls of your antivirus software and begin turning the knobs. Go ahead; show your antivirus software who's boss!

Setting Your Computer Boot Options

In this section I talk you through the configuration settings associated with your computer's startup sequence. These are important options because you need to be assured that your computer is free of Master Boot Record (MBR) and boot sector viruses (viruses that reside not in files but in the hard drive's master boot record or a floppy disk's boot sector). Also, you want your antivirus program to automatically start up when your computer starts so that protection against viruses begins the minute your computer is up and running.

I can tell you from personal experience that although I'm a diligent and experienced computer user, sometimes I forget to do even the most routine tasks on my computer. If I had to rely on my memory to start my antivirus program, I'm sure I'd have been smitten a number of times over the years. (Good thing all my body parts are permanently attached, or I'd forget them, too. Let's not go there.)

Antivirus program starts at computer's startup

The option that starts your antivirus software as soon as your computer boots up is nonnegotiable. You've *got* to have your antivirus program start up automatically. Depending on which version of Windows you're using — and which brand of antivirus software you have — this could mean that the antivirus program is up and running even before you get to the login prompt. This is a very good thing: You want your antivirus program running as soon as possible. Figure 5-1 shows the startup options available in the McAfee VirusScan suite (note the automatic-startup option in the first check box).

Scanning computer memory

Like starting at bootup (which I describe above), memory scanning is another nonnegotiable item, even though every brand of antivirus software handles this feature a bit differently. For sure you want your antivirus program to scan your computer's memory, because some viruses are *memory-resident* — that means the little monster will quietly sit in your computer's memory, licking its chops and waiting for unwitting victims to ensnare — or perhaps it just snoozes until its little alarm clock goes off, and then . . . boom!

Anyway, some antivirus programs will scan your computer's memory at startup, in case any viruses are lurking there. If your particular antivirus program displays this characteristic as an option, then you should definitely turn this option on.

Further, some products permit you to scan your computer's memory on demand, much like you would scan a file, directory, or floppy disk. Figure 5-2 illustrates this capability.

Scanning floppy disks and CD-ROMs

One nice characteristic of some antivirus programs is that they can scan any removable media for viruses when your computer is shutting down — whether your computer is restarting or going down entirely. If this option is available in your antivirus program, you should enable it.

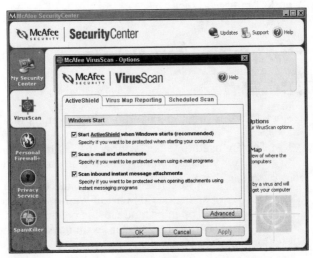

Figure 5-1: Automatic start at boot time is a must-have feature.

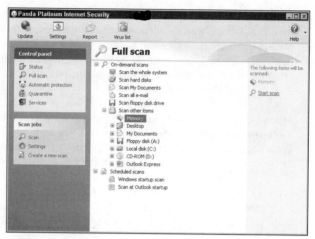

Figure 5-2: Some antivirus products permit you to scan memory on demand.

Here is why scanning removable media is important: If you are restarting your computer, and if your computer has a bootable floppy disk or CD-ROM inserted, then — depending on your computer's configuration — your computer may restart itself from the floppy disk or CD-ROM. If the floppy disk or CD-ROM has a boot-sector virus, then your computer could become infected with that virus before the antivirus program has an opportunity to detect it.

Configuring Automatic Protection

Most antivirus programs operate in two primary modes:

✔ They're used to "scan" your entire computer (or a part of it) for viruses that may already be present there.

✔ They're used to actively monitor your computer's activities — in particular, that part of Windows that controls the creating, opening, and closing of computer files — so the antivirus program can examine each active file for signs of a virus.

The latter function is automatic, and it has a variety of names. Symantec calls it *Auto-Protect* (the Auto-Protect configuration screen is shown in Figure 5-3), while McAfee uses the term *ActiveShield*. But whatever the name, the function is the same: Your antivirus program is actively *preventing* a file with a virus from being implanted in your computer in the first place. This is a Very Good Thing™.

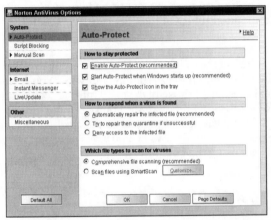

Figure 5-3: Automatic protection is a beneficial feature.

Scheduling Scans

Having your antivirus program scan the entire computer for viruses is a necessity. Even though most antivirus programs have an auto-protect feature that should — theoretically — prevent the insertion of a virus onto your computer, it's *still* a good idea to scan your computer periodically in the event something was missed somehow by the automatic protection.

I recommend that you scan your computer once per week. But (as I've said elsewhere in this book) if you're like me and prone to forgetfulness, then you need to have your computer do your remembering for you — and do its weekly scan on its own.

When to scan

When scheduling periodic scans, choose a day and time when you know your computer will be running. It's no good to schedule a scan for Friday night at 10:00 p.m. if your computer is turned off. The antivirus program will *not* wake up your computer if it isn't running — but if it's already running, then it doesn't need to be awakened. (Oh, I think you know what I mean.)

If your computer is in standby or hibernation mode (common battery-saving modes on laptops), your antivirus program will *not* wake it up to scan. It's got to be fully awake and running at the appointed time. On the plus side, your monitor needn't be on.

One other factor to take into account for your weekly scan: Run it when your computer is running but when you're *not* using it. If you have one of those high-speed Internet connections (such as cable or DSL), then perhaps you keep your computer on all the time anyway. If so, then you can just schedule your scan to take place, say, on Fridays at 1:00 a.m. (or whenever you're routinely *not* using the computer).

Manual or automatic?

If you turn your computer off when you're not using it, then you may need to change your habits a little bit — if you can get beyond the hassle — so the scan can run when you're not using the computer.

But why make a fuss about running a virus scan when you're *not* using the computer? Well, the computer needs all its resources to do the scan efficiently. If you're using your computer for just about *anything* else while a virus scan is running, it's generally *not* a fun experience. A virus scan makes your computer dog-slow, miserably-slow, because the scanning program has to examine each of the 20,000–50,000 files on your computer, checking every one for any of the 60,000+ known viruses. That is a *lot* of work for the computer to do.

If you really want to see for yourself, I suggest you run a virus scan while you're using your computer for something else. Within moments, if your experience is like mine, your computer will be running very slowly. Watching eternity wear away while your commands try to get a word in edgewise.

If your computer is generally turned on only while you're using it (and only then), you have a choice to make: Either you need to scan the computer while you're using it, or you need to change your work habits to accommodate the scan. For instance, turn on your computer first thing in the morning, and run the virus scan while you're off taking a shower, eating a meal, meeting with other people, practicing the accordion, or whatever. Or run the scan at some other time when the computer is on but you're not using it for anything *but* the scan. (Siesta, anyone?)

What to scan

Thankfully, figuring out *what* to scan is easier than knowing *when* to scan. Here's what this means: The antivirus program can be configured to scan different *types* of files. A file's *type* is determined by the last three letters of the file's *name*. For example, the file scanlog.txt is a *text* file, because the last three letters of the file's name (called its *extension*) are txt, meaning *text file*. A file ending in .EXE is a program — or *executable* — file, and a file ending in .CAB is a *cabinet file,* a special kind of archive file used by Windows.

There are dozens — even hundreds or thousands — of file types in use today. But the good news is that you don't need to know all these different file types. Why? Simple: *The best thing is to scan all types of files!* That's right: If you scan *every* type of file that there is now, or ever will be in the future, then you're 100 percent covered.

Fortunately, most antivirus programs do this comprehensive scan by default, but they still give you a choice. This is because a long time ago in a galaxy far, far away, viruses only infected .EXE and .COM file types, so scanning only those was all you needed to do. But then other types of viruses came along, and you had to scan more and more types of files, until the antivirus program makers got smart and added the option, scan *all* types of files. So this option to specify which types of file to scan is sort of a leftover from those earlier days.

You can, however, also tell your antivirus program which types of files *not* to scan — an exclusion list. But for the vast majority of readers, you do not need to tell your antivirus program which types of files to skip. You can just leave this blank.

System Restore can restore viruses

Starting with Windows XP Professional, Microsoft introduced a new feature in Windows that gives us another "out" in case we experience computer problems. System Restore is used to "roll back" the operating system to a known working state. System Restore only touches the operating system, not your files, so System Restore doesn't roll *everything* back, just the operating system changes.

So if your computer catches a virus, the virus will be archived in the System Restore repository, out of reach of antivirus programs. You can unwittingly set the virus free from its prison if you find that you have to restore your system to an earlier known-working state with System Restore. A virus that may have been snuffed out is suddenly alive on your computer again!

What to do? First, if you have to do a System Restore, I suggest you immediately scan your entire computer for viruses, in case you brought one back from the grave. Next, refer to your antivirus program's Web site for updates, in the event that its makers figure out how to scan the System Restore repository.

Scheduling Updates

Next to scheduling scans, scheduling *virus-signature updates* is one of the most important ways to use your antivirus program. Getting updates is what your antivirus program does when it needs to get information on all of the latest viruses. It is important to keep your antivirus program up to date in order to stop any of the *new* viruses that are circulating around.

Most human beings don't remember to do these updates — or have better things to do than chase all over the Internet looking for new virus signatures. This is why antivirus programs let you specify how often to do the updates automatically. Then the antivirus program can go and do the updates all by itself without your having to remember.

How you connect to the Internet

Your antivirus program needs to know how you connect to the Internet. If you have a high-speed cable modem or DSL connection, you would tell the antivirus program that you have a "direct" connection.

If, on the other hand, you're a twentieth-century throwback who uses dial-up access to connect to the Internet, I promise not to tell, but you do have a bit more configuring to do. (Flip over to Chapter 4 for a refresher on how your computer connects to the Internet.)

How often to update

How frequently you will need to update your antivirus definitions depends on three factors:

- ✔ **The nature of your Internet connection.** Is it dial-up? DSL? Cable? If it's one of the latter (or another variety of high-speed connection), update frequently.

- ✔ **How vital your computer is to you.** Do you use it to make your living? If you do (or if it performs some other function that you can't do without), update frequently.

- ✔ **What kinds of activities you perform on your computer.** Do you receive great bogs of e-mail every day? You guessed it: Update frequently.

If you use dial-up connectivity, do only a little e-mail, use Web-based mail (where your service provider may be scanning your messages for you), or mostly use your computer for entertainment, then you can update less frequently. (Hard-core gamers, conversely, may want take into consideration the amount of time they've invested in working up to demigod level in their favorite computer game and update a bit more frequently, as well.)

So, how often to update? Well, after you assess the level of risk you're comfortable with, you can follow the guidelines in Table 5-1.

Table 5-1	How Often to Update Virus Signatures
How Often to Update	*Your Usage Patterns*
Every three days	Dial-up connection to the Internet
	Low volume of e-mail
	Hobby and entertainment
Every day	Dial-up or high-speed Internet connection
	More e-mail
	Some file sharing
Every four hours	High-speed, "always-on" Internet connection
	High volume of e-mail
	Lots of file sharing

If your computer activities are high-risk and/or high-value, then it makes sense to update the antivirus signatures more frequently. If this is important to you, then you should be sure to choose an antivirus product that lets you specify how frequently it will check for updates.

Unlike scanning your computer for viruses, updates are fairly low-impact. If you have a high-speed "always on" connection, you could update your virus definitions every hour if you like. In fact, if your usage patterns entailed lower risk (say, if you have a low volume of e-mail, or use the computer for hobbies and entertainment), you could still update as frequently as every hour if you have a high-speed, always-on connection. Why not? The antivirus software company does not limit how frequently you are permitted to check for updates, so it's really up to you.

If you are still not sure how often to update your virus signatures, generally you'll be fine as long as you update at least once each week. It's better to check for updates more frequently, but more frequently than every hour or two is overkill.

If you're still wavering, set your antivirus program to update once per day. Don't be too surprised if you feel better afterward.

Configuring Heuristics

Heuristics? Huh? Well, no, it doesn't mean running in panicky circles. But it plays a role in virus detection because of two factors:

- ✔ **Viruses are created all the time — over twenty new ones each day.** Even if your antivirus program checks for virus-signature updates very frequently, there is still some risk that you can catch a virus before your antivirus company creates a signature for it.

- ✔ **Most viruses exhibit predictable behavior patterns.** There are a number of things that most viruses do that the antivirus companies are very familiar with.

These two factors have led the antivirus companies to employ a new way of detecting viruses — by carefully observing the Windows operating system for the typical patterns that most viruses exhibit. For instance, many viruses attempt to attach themselves to program files. The antivirus program can watch for this type of behavior and block it. This method detects viruses by observing their effects, as opposed to checking files for matches against the virus-signature file.

If the antivirus program you're using has such a *heuristics* setting, it would be a good idea to turn it on. You never know when you might be unfortunate enough to catch a virus, especially one that is so new that your antivirus maker hasn't made an entry for your signature file yet. Heuristics can make your computer much safer.

When a new virus is released, many people fall victim before the virus is captured by any of the antivirus companies. Anyone can be such a target, and heuristics is the only thing available to stop new viruses. Or, you could just turn off your computer (yeah, right).

Configuring E-Mail Protection

Because e-mail is one of the chief means of transporting viruses, most antivirus programs have options that help them work with your e-mail program. This only applies when you are using a "local" e-mail program to read and send mail, and not when you are using a Web browser to handle your mail.

The options that you'll most likely see are used to specify whether your antivirus program should scan incoming mail messages, and whether it should scan outgoing mail messages. If you see such options, you should turn them on.

Your antivirus program might install buttons in your e-mail program that permit you to scan specific messages (or all messages) in the inbox or another mail folder. There could also be a button installed on e-mail that will let you open your antivirus program right from within your e-mail program.

Configuring Instant Messaging Protection

As instant messaging (IM) rises in popularity, it has become the new way for viruses to jump from computer to computer. Consequently, it would be nice if your antivirus program was aware of your IM activity so it could watch for any suspicious activity indicative of a virus.

Configuration for IM in your antivirus program may be no more than a check box or two. Does the antivirus program watch IM or not? If it can, I recommend that you tell it to do so. (After all, you've paid for some protection, right?)

Chapter 6

Scanning Your Computer and E-Mail

• •

In This Chapter

▶ Understanding the role of virus scanning

▶ Convincing yourself (well, we can hope) to scan for viruses

▶ Performing a manual virus scan

▶ Setting up a schedule for scans

▶ Considering Web-based scanning tools

▶ Scanning e-mail

• •

*I*n this chapter, I help you scan your computer and e-mail for viruses. This is an essential chore that you've got to do on a regular basis in order to ensure that your computer is free of viruses. In many cases, you can configure your antivirus program to automatically perform this scan as often as necessary. Because this feature can save you time and trouble, I show you how to make the necessary configuration choices in Chapter 5.

I also show you how to manually scan the e-mail in your mailbox. Some antivirus programs include this feature; it's a convenient way to double-check the cleanliness of your inbox.

Deciding to Scan Your Computer File-by-File

Scanning your computer doesn't ring up its price, and you needn't concern yourself with the age-old dilemma, *paper or plastic?* But directing your antivirus software to conduct a thorough file-by-file *scan* (or search) of your computer using an updated virus *signature file* (like a book of virus finger-prints) is the second half of your antivirus software's one-two punch against viruses. Permit me to explain.

Antivirus programs use two main methods to detect viruses:

✓ **Automatic protection:** Antivirus programs can (and do) carefully watch all of your computer's hard drive activity while you're doing whatever you do on your computer. If your computer is about to copy a file containing a virus to the hard drive (or floppy, or CD-ROM), the antivirus program will detect this and immediately intervene to block the action. For the scoop on configuring automatic protection and heuristics, see Chapter 5.

✓ **Scanning:** A scan is different from real-time protection. A scan is a one-time file-by-file examination of your entire computer — sort of a house-by-house search — looking for viruses that may be hiding inside of a program or document.

You can also do a scan of removable media such as floppy disks and CD-ROMs before you use them. And if you're in an environment that has a file server (which *should* have its own antivirus program), you can scan files on the server.

The automatic real-time method for detecting viruses, which I explain in the previous section, isn't 100-percent reliable. I'm not implying that there is something wrong with antivirus programs. But there are some ways that viruses can circumvent your antivirus defenses.

If you scan your entire computer say, every week, on the other hand, then by the time your next weekly scan occurs, chances are that your antivirus program will have downloaded a new virus definition that includes a signature for the new virus. The weekly scan will then detect the virus that the automatic detector missed.

Your antivirus program actually can be circumvented in two ways:

✓ **New or unknown viruses:** Your antivirus program can only stop viruses that it knows about. If a brand-new virus pops up on the Internet, it's possible (though not really *likely*) that it will get to your computer before your antivirus company can get a virus definition file with the new virus's signature into your computer.

If your computer gets one of these brand-new viruses, it could also be spreading the virus to other computers without your knowing it. Not a good way to treat friends. (And what if they find out that *you* are sending them viruses?)

✔ **Computer malfunctions:** A computer malfunction can also make it vulnerable to viruses. For instance, perhaps your antivirus program had some kind of a strange problem that caused it to stop watching for viruses in its "real-time" module. The antivirus program might get sick on its own accord, or a malfunction elsewhere in the computer's hardware or software might cause it to freak out and stop working. Not a way to start your day.

A *user* malfunction can invite troubles, too. One thing I've seen a few times is a situation where the installation procedure for a new program asks you to temporarily disable your automatic virus protection to prevent it from interfering with the installation. If you forget to reactivate your antivirus program's automatic protection, then any virus — new and old — can walk right in if it gets the chance.

Scanning for Viruses

I explain in the previous section *why* scans are needed, so in this section, I present the *how* side of the equation. You have choices about how you scan your computer. You can scan automatically or manually, and, within manual scans, you can scan your entire computer or you can scan one file, one directory, the CD-ROM drive, and so on.

In Chapter 5, I explain how to configure your antivirus program to automatically scan your entire computer. Put your thumb on this page and go to Chapter 5 to see how to set up those automatic scans.

You can also manually scan your entire computer — or just a part of it — any time you like. Stick with me in the following sections to see how to manage a manual scan.

Why does scanning take so long?

Scanning your entire hard drive could take an hour or longer. This depends upon many factors, including:

- ✔ The speed of your computer's processor
- ✔ The size of your hard drive
- ✔ The speed of your hard drive
- ✔ The number of files on your hard drive
- ✔ The extent of fragmentation on your hard drive
- ✔ Your patience

So it's hard to say how long it *should* take, but here's why it takes so long. . . .

There are over 60,000 known viruses today, and your antivirus program has "signatures" on each one of them in your computer's virus definition file. When your antivirus program scans for viruses, it opens each of the over-ten-thousand files on your computer, and examines each one for the presence of all of these viruses.

Frankly, given the sheer size of this task, I am amazed that virus scanning is so *fast!*

Scanning the entire computer

The *brute-force* method of scanning your computer is to look at the entire hard drive and every file in it. It's actually pretty easy to tell your antivirus software to do this — just scan drive C:, or *all hard drives,* or however your antivirus program offers the choices to you.

There are probably ten thousand or more files on your computer, and probably many times more than that. Your antivirus software is meticulous and actually enjoys examining every blade of grass in the field. Not much else to do, I guess.

To scan your entire computer for viruses, follow these steps:

1. **Open your antivirus program and run the Scan command.**

   Each program is a bit different, but the Scan command is usually a button or hyperlink toward the top of the main interface screen.

2. **Select the drive letter that corresponds to your computer's hard drive.**

Most programs give you a choice of which drive letter to scan.

If your computer's hard drive is divided into two or more drive letters, you'll need to scan each one. And likewise, if your computer has more than one hard drive, then you'll need to scan each one. It's possible, though, that your antivirus program has an *All Hard Drives* option, which makes this easier. Then, somewhere, you'll find a *Start Scan* (or *Begin, Go, Giddyup,* whatever) button to get the scan started.

Figure 6-1 shows a scan in progress using Panda Antivirus Platinum.

Scanning a file or directory

Most antivirus programs, in addition to letting you scan your entire computer for viruses, also give you the ability to scan individual files and directories.

Some antivirus programs require you to open the antivirus program, select the *scan* option, and then browse to the file(s) or directory(ies) you wish to scan. This *works,* but it's not all that convenient.

Other antivirus programs have gone a step further: They have integrated their program right into Windows Explorer so you can right-click a file or directory and select the Scan for Viruses option without having to open your antivirus program at all. Cool huh?! See Figure 6-2 for an example of this.

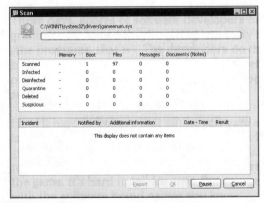

Figure 6-1: A virus scan in progress.

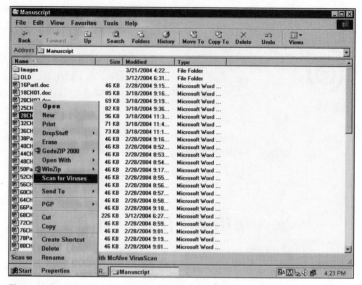

Figure 6-2: Scanning for viruses from within Windows Explorer.

How often to scan

As I mention in Chapter 5, you need to periodically scan your entire computer for viruses if you want to be completely sure that your computer is virus-free. For a number of reasons, your antivirus program's real-time virus protection is not infallible. (I hope you're not getting tired of me making this point. Viruses are *so* much more tiresome.)

But how often is *often enough?* If I were forced to give a general answer to fit most users' purposes, I would have to say that scanning your entire computer for viruses once per week is about right.

Some of you, though, should scan more frequently; it depends on what you do with your computer. For instance, if you make your living on your computer by day-trading stocks, getting rich (yeah right) on eBay, or writing *For Dummies* books, then you have a lot more to lose than if you do a little e-mail and surf the Net now and then. So the economic value of your computer may prompt you to scan more often for viruses.

If you are engaged in doing a lot of downloads or file sharing (the legal kind, of course), or you have a habit of opening the attachments in e-mail messages from people you don't know (and I have some *can't-miss* land in Florida to sell you if you do), then you are increasing your risk of catching a virus. If you fall into this high-risk group, then you've got to scan your computer more often to be sure that your computer is virus-free.

Scheduling Scans

Because whole-computer scans take so long and make your computer so sluggish, you might schedule your computer to do its scans at a regular time when you're not using it. Personally, I have my antivirus program scan my entire computer on Mondays at 1:00 a.m. Sometimes I stay up late on the computer on Sunday nights, but never *that* late. On my computer, the scan takes two or three hours, so even if I get up really early on Monday morning, the scan is usually done by the time I'm back on the computer.

You should think of a good time when your computer is always on (this is harder on laptop computers as many of us put them on "standby" or "hibernate" when we're not using them) and schedule the scan for a time when you're not using it. This is just my personal preference. It's also possible that the newest and very fastest computers can better handle a full-computer virus scan while running heavyweight software such as Internet Explorer (a little sarcasm there) at the same time.

Evaluating Online Scanning Services

Some well-known makes of antivirus software have introduced Web-based virus scanning. You can go to one of these Web sites and click the <u>Scan my computer for viruses</u> link. The Web page downloads a small program that will then scan your entire computer for viruses — usually for free (such a deal!).

While there are some drawbacks to this approach, it can be quite useful in some situations. For instance, you could do one of these scans on a computer that *doesn't* have antivirus software, or whose antivirus software isn't working at the moment. It's also potentially useful to permit a second program (the online scanner in this case) to have a look at your computer to see if your computer is *really* free of viruses.

Some of the online scanning programs will remove a virus if they detect one, while others can detect but not remove. Depending upon your motivation, you might choose one online scanning tool over another. Or, you could try a different one each time. Figure 6-3 shows a popular online virus-scanning tool.

Personally, I think that the online scanning tools exist for promotional reasons. When an online scanning tool finds a virus, could easily say something like, "Saaaay, I've found a virus here, but you'll have to *buy* our antivirus product at full price in order to fix it." Ka-ching! Sarcasm aside, these online scanning tools have their usefulness.

Can online scan programs be trusted?

Okay, call me paranoid (hah! that's what *they* want you to believe. . . .). But as an information-security professional, I find that paranoia — well, *caution* — is a trait that leads to a long and productive career in this business. In this day and age, how can one be sure that the online virus-scanning tool is doing what it's supposed to, and nothing else?

Personally, I put more trust in an antivirus program that I buy at the local computer retailer than I do in an online virus-scanning program. But only a *tiny* bit more.

True, you have to have *faith* to connect to the Internet, and you have to have some level of trust just to use the Internet. So I'll compromise and tell you this: You can trust the online scanning tools offered by the major antivirus makers, as long as

- ✔ You have security patches installed (one or more patches have addressed the problem associated with knowing what Web site you are actually visiting).

- ✔ You do *not* visit the online scan Web page by clicking a URL in an unsolicited mail message. You do *not* want to be a victim of one of those "phishing" scams! (I talk about phishing scams and other sleazy tricks in Chapter 14.)

- ✔ You do not use Phil and George's Most Excellent Online Virus Scanning Tool and Mail-Order Sushi to scan your computer. Stick with reputable brands.

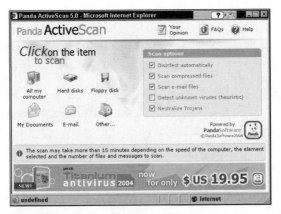

Figure 6-3: Panda online virus scan.

Scanning E-mail

I know that some readers are going to wonder whether their antivirus software automatically scans incoming mail messages for viruses. If your antivirus software has automatic virus detection, then yes, your antivirus program will automatically scan each inbound message for viruses.

However, there are some additional features found on some antivirus programs when used with some local e-mail programs. Specifically, you could find that your e-mail program has a Scan for Antivirus button on the toolbar (as shown in Figure 6-4), where you can select one or more messages and scan all of those selected messages for viruses.

This is like a manual scan for viruses, except that this scanning can be done from inside of your e-mail program. Presumably your antivirus program already scanned all of the messages in your inbox when they arrived. But, if a new virus is on the loose, and you've just been able to download the latest virus signature database that includes this new virus, then scanning messages you already have would tell you whether any of those messages have this brand-new virus.

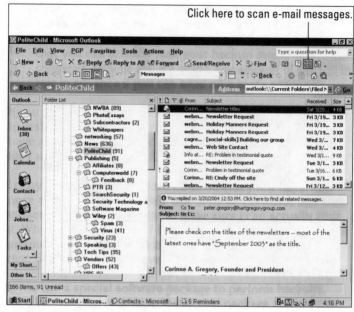

Click here to scan e-mail messages.

Figure 6-4: Some antivirus programs place a button in your e-mail program.

I won't go so far as to recommend that you manually rescan all of your mail for new viruses. But if you are among the legion of the ultra-careful (whose only worry is whether they're paranoid *enough*), then by all means rescan your e-mail from time to time; a clean computer is a balm to the worried mind.

By default, the regular periodic scan of your entire computer also scans your e-mail. The reason that your e-mail is also scanned is that the mail messages on your computer are stored in files on the hard drive, just like your documents, programs, and other stuff. The scan-your-e-mail button is available more for your convenience (for example, by allowing you to scan *only* your e-mail rather than the entire hard drive) than as a necessity.

Here is a useful example of the capability to scan messages from within your e-mail program: Before opening certain e-mail messages, you could re-scan messages if you think there is *any* possibility of their harboring a virus.

Scanning outbound e-mail

The preceding section deals primarily with scanning incoming mail, but what about mail that you are *sending?* Does your antivirus program automatically scan it for viruses? Viruses and their writers are pretty sneaky; if your antivirus program scans files as they are created (the "automatic" protection), then you can be sure that outbound mail is virus-free.

That said, however, many antivirus programs do have a specific module that is "hooked in" to your e-mail program (again, just the "local" e-mail kinds like Outlook Express and Eudora) to scan each outbound message before it gets out of your computer. If you use Web-based e-mail, your ISP may be scanning your outbound mail automatically.

This is a good feature, because some e-mail programs don't write your outbound messages to the hard drive until after they are sent. A plain-Jane antivirus program that is not e-mail aware would catch the virus, but only after your mail program had sent it out. This is precisely the reason why good antivirus programs specifically hook into your local e-mail program in order to detect and block outgoing viruses.

Detecting viruses in e-mail

So what are you supposed to do if your antivirus program catches a virus in an incoming mail message? It depends.

What's worse than e-mail spam? How about *spam with a virus attached?* Spam filters watch for spammers' favorite words — so spammers use a bizarre mishmash language to get past the filters. In fact, that's one clue to watch for. If the message containing the virus was from 984Jiel3Z@yahoo. com and the subject line was something like hello, Free ca.ble d3sc4ambl3r, or RE: horseman antacid driving cobalt — in other words, if it's spam — then you do nothing. Above all, *don't open the message;* just delete it and move on. Don't waste your time with such messages. Save your curiosity for other purposes.

If, on the other hand, the virus is in a message sent from someone you know, then think before you reply. True, you at least owe that person the courtesy of letting him or her know that a virus-infected e-mail message came to you from that address. This stuff happens, and perhaps it's happened to you in the past. But wait a minute.

Some viruses grab all the addresses in an infected computer's e-mail address book and then send infected messages to every address. It's possible that your friend did not *knowingly* send you an infected message. In fact, your friend may not even be the person from whose computer the message was sent. Some viruses use a stolen return address from one computer as the fake return address for infected messages sent from a *different* infected computer.

Suppose, for example, you have a friend named Jane (not her real name). One day you receive an infected e-mail message that appears to have been sent from Jane. However, things are often not as they seem. Another person, named Bob (not his real name), did catch a virus from someone, and the virus sent out lots of e-mail messages. You and Jane are in Bob's e-mail address book, and the virus created a message to send to you from Bob's computer, with Jane's return address.

So in this example, Bob's computer sent you an infected message that *appears* to have been sent from Jane, but in reality Jane had nothing to do with it. So if you send mail to Jane to tell her that she may have a virus, she may not know what you're talking about — but she should probably check anyway.

It is for this reason that you need to be wary of messages in your inbox that appear to have been sent from people you know. You can't judge a mail message by its subject line.

Viruses are doing tricky things like this in order to spread chaos, confusion, and mistrust. *Thems tricksy virus writers! We hates them, we do!*

Chapter 7

Ridding Your Computer of Viruses

● ●

In This Chapter

▶ Figuring out the meaning of warning messages

▶ Locating quarantined files

▶ Fixing the damage done to your system

● ●

*T*here's a virus in your computer, or at least you're pretty sure there is. You'll find out how to tell the difference and know what to do if it looks like there really is a virus in there somewhere.

If you think there is a virus on your computer, but you're not really sure, flip over to Chapter 6 and find out for sure. Come on back here when you're done. The rest of us aren't going anywhere — except on a virus hunt.

Interpreting Warning Messages

You may have seen a warning message that appeared to come from your antivirus program — and said it found a virus. First response: Separate fact from fiction.

If your message was wholly contained within an e-mail message, then it's most likely a "spam" (junk) message, and one of two things is going on:

✔ Someone may be trying to trick you into visiting a Web site where you can *really* get infected with something.

✔ Someone may be trying to get you to input your credit-card number, whether for some legitimate or (often) illegitimate reason.

Both unsavory tricks are typical. If you're not sure, you may want to grab a copy of *Fighting Spam For Dummies* (also from Wiley) and look into it further.

Bottom line: If the message comes from a stranger and your e-mail program shows an attachment, *don't open the message or the attachment* until you're pretty sure of what you're dealing with.

Warnings about incoming e-mail

Different antivirus programs have different ways of showing you when a virus is detected in an e-mail message. Some slip a note into the mail message, informing you that your program has removed a virus from a particular mail message. Others warn you with a pop-up window (not a *browser* pop-up, but one produced by your antivirus program) when they detect a virus in a mail message.

Most of the time, the antivirus program removes the virus and fixes things on the spot, says so, and there's nothing further to worry about. Your antivirus program functions as judge, jury, and executioner all in one (when you see a message along the lines of what's shown in Figure 7-1, you can breathe easily).

But sometimes your antivirus program can't remove the virus — especially if the virus is too new — so you've got to become familiar with how your antivirus program tells you what's up. If it can kill the inbound virus — and does so and tells you so — then you've got nothing further to worry about. If (sinister music here) your antivirus program *detects but can't remove* the virus, three burning questions crop up:

✔ If it detects a virus but can't kill it, does that mean my system is already infected (and should I panic now)?

✔ If my system *isn't* infected, how can I dispose of the virus without launching it (what's my equivalent of oven mitts)?

✔ What do I do now? (Scream? Use bad language? Pitch my computer and move to a cave?)

Well (for openers), if you find yourself in the situation in which the antivirus software can't remove the virus, go right to the section in this chapter called "Repairing Your System." If not, no problem — chill out and read on.

Figure 7-1: An e-mail virus has been found and eradicated.

Warnings about incoming files

It began innocently enough: You were copying files to your computer from a CD-ROM, DVD-ROM, or even a floppy disk (let's hear it for classic tech!) — or you were downloading from the Internet or over a network from some other computer — when suddenly a shot rang out. Oops, wrong story — *when suddenly your antivirus program put up a window* telling you it just found a virus, something like the window shown in Figure 7-2.

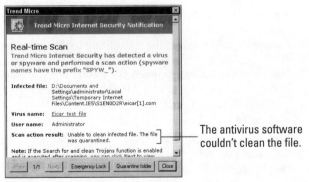

The antivirus software couldn't clean the file.

Figure 7-2: A warning message tells you that a virus has been found.

Don't put off repairs

If your computer has a virus, you should not do anything on your computer (other than your search-and-destroy mission) until you are sure that the virus is gone. If you are hoping it'll go away or are pretending it's gone, you're kidding yourself. The longer you put off eradicating the virus, the worse off you may become. Some viruses even try to turn your system into a modern-day Typhoid Mary, spreading infection to dozens, hundreds, or even thousands of other computer users on the Internet. Baaaad Karma. Until the virus is gone, you risk the possibility that files or programs on your computer will be damaged, and that you will spread the virus to others. 'Nuff said.

Take a close look at the message from your antivirus program. It's telling you that it found a virus and *can* fix (remove) it, or that it found a virus and *cannot* fix or remove it. What comes next depends on what it told you.

Fixed

If your antivirus program did catch and crush the virus, then you have *almost* nothing to worry about. You *do* know that some particular file that you were reading, copying, or downloading had a virus in it. You also know that your antivirus program *did* detect it and prevent it from causing any damage to your computer, and also that it prevented it from spreading from your computer to other computers. But does it end there?

You may feel an obligation to inform the file's owner(s) that it has a virus. But then again, perhaps they *do* know. You have a judgment call to make; the right thing to do varies by situation.

However — you've now seen your antivirus program doing its job: It detected a virus and killed it on the spot.

Not fixed

If your antivirus program tells you that it couldn't clean the file, then you have some more work to do. Probably, one of two things is going on:

> ✔ **Your program detected the virus, but could not remove it from the file.** Don't head for the hills yet; you are still

probably quite safe. In situations like this, the antivirus program is not going to just leave you vulnerable; instead, it completely removes the infected file (either by deleting it or placing it in quarantine) so the virus contained in it can't hurt you. (Gives *me* warm fuzzies, how about you?)

✔ **Your program detected a virus but couldn't zap it, and the file that carries the virus is lurking on your system.** Check out the "Repairing Your System" section of this chapter.

Warnings resulting from a virus scan

Whoops, there it is: You scan your computer for viruses, and the scan finds a virus that sneaked in. You've got a "situation" on your hands. The first thing you should be asking yourself is, *How did the infected file slip past the real-time virus detection and get itself into your computer?*

There are a couple of possible explanations that are not particularly alarming, but you're not out of the woods yet:

✔ The virus may be so new that it entered your computer before your antivirus program had a "signature" for it.

✔ Real-time virus detection was (and still may be) turned off at the time the virus entered your computer.

✔ Your antivirus software has no real-time virus detection.

Whatever your situation, your computer has a virus. It entered your computer and parked itself in a file somewhere. What we don't know (and it's pretty close to impossible to find out in many cases) is whether the virus "activated" and performed whatever evil deeds it was designed to do. The virus may still be "sleeping," waiting for a date (a specific day on the calendar, not a night out with a virus of the opposite parity), or waiting for some other condition.

Take note of the name of the virus — its entire name. You've got some research to do. You'll need to visit the antivirus program's Web site and read about this particular virus to see what it does to victims' computers (the really nice antivirus programs, when they display the message telling you about the virus, may have a "click here for more information" button that takes you right to information on this particular virus, as shown in Figure 7-3). After getting the word, you'll be wise to look for signs of this specific activity, whatever it may be.

If you have any repair work to do, skip ahead in this chapter to "Repairing Your System."

Only after you get all the way through these few steps can you be sure that the virus is really gone. But to be sure, it's wise to do another scan.

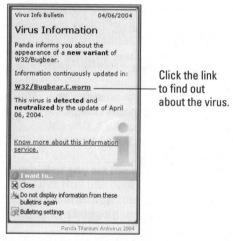

Click the link to find out about the virus.

Figure 7-3: Panda Antivirus provides a convenient link to information about a virus.

Finding Quarantined Files

Because computer viruses behave like viruses in the organic world (in the way that they infect and spread), it's no wonder some medical terms crossed over into the computer world. For example, antivirus programs borrowed *quarantine* from hospitals, where it's a secure place (and a set of procedures) intended to isolate patients with infectious diseases so they don't infect other patients or hospital workers. On your computer, it's a usually a subdirectory (created for this purpose when your antivirus program was installed) that serves as somewhere to put a file infected with a virus. Any contact with the infected file is limited for safety's sake. (Nope, there are no visiting hours.)

Files in quarantine are there for one of two reasons:

- ✓ **It's the original file version:** The files there may be the infected versions of files that were successfully repaired. Repaired files will be found in their original locations.

- ✓ **It's the only file version:** For files that could not be repaired, the quarantine is the *only* place where they can be found.

The antivirus program, in cahoots with the operating system, may prevent you from accessing quarantined files. If you find yourself with quarantined files, you may be limited to just looking at them through a heavy plate-glass window.

 Different antivirus programs handle quarantine access differently — if you've gotten lost in the quarantine cave, the antivirus program's help info will guide you and let you know what you can and can't do with the file.

Repairing Your System

If you encounter a pop-up message from your antivirus program telling you that you have a virus, then you're in the right place. Regardless of the means your antivirus program used to spot your virus, you should write down the exact name(s) of the virus(es) that it found, and the file that was infected. Then it's time to start bailing water.

Determining the extent of the damage

Determining how much mayhem a virus has wrought is an important task because the things you may need to do are determined by your fact-finding. The procedure here is actually pretty simple:

1. **Identify which virus (or viruses) your computer has.**

   Write down their names; know thy enemy.

2. **Go to your antivirus program's Web site and find out more about the virus.**

Most such Web sites have a feature that provides
details about particular viruses: what they do, where
they hide, and what it takes to get rid of 'em.

3. **Read the description carefully.**

   Try to understand what — if any — damage the virus
   may have done to your computer.

4. **Check the antivirus program's Web site to see
   whether it suggests a specific virus-removal tool.**

   The Web site may further describe damage that the
   virus is known to do and whether you need to take
   any more action.

   Well, no, you don't have to memorize chapter and verse
   on the precise nature of the damage, but look for the
   types of damage that the virus is known to inflict. Does
   it (for example) infect specific parts of your operating
   system? Corrupt files? Destroy access to data?

The antivirus companies are generally pretty good about
explaining exactly how to determine whether any damage has
occurred. The *good* antivirus companies will give easy-to-
understand instructions that practically anyone will be able to
understand and follow.

Repairing damage

The range of possible virus mayhem is too vast to get really
specific here. A typical Windows system has thousands of
files, any of which could be the victim of the virus — whether
by being removed, renamed, altered, or corrupted. Or one or
more of *your* files may have been the target of the virus. I'll be
rather general here and describe the likely categories of repair.

Getting and running a repair program

Sometimes the virus that your computer is infected with
can't be completely eradicated from your computer with the
means in your antivirus program. If this is the case, then your
antivirus software company may have a repair program that
you can download and run.

Before you download and run the repair program, it's important that you read all the way through any instructions and
notes. Given how tricky viruses can be these days, just running

the repair program may not be enough. You may need to do something *before* you run the repair program, and maybe even something else *afterward.*

If you're a bit anxious, that's natural. You can get a good start by downloading the needed program. I suggest you save the program to your computer before running it (you may need to run it a second time, or use it on another computer, for instance).

 Read through the steps completely before beginning. If you don't feel confident that you can handle the instructions, enlist the help of an expert friend or take your computer in for repair. In some cases, a mistake can cause additional damage to your computer over and above what the virus may have done.

Reinstalling files

Some viruses remove one or more files from the Windows operating system. Your antivirus program's Web site may have specific instructions on where to get this file, and perhaps they even have a copy you can get right from their Web site.

Then again, you may need to get the information (or even the fix) from Microsoft. If this is the case, your antivirus company should have precise instructions that tell you exactly where and how to get it. I'd be surprised if your antivirus company left you out in the cold.

Be careful, and go slowly. Computers are intolerant of mistakes; they do just what you *tell* them to do, not what you *meant* for them to do.

Booting from a rescue disk

If you are unable to boot your computer at all, it's possible that your computer has become infected with a boot sector virus that is interfering with the computer's boot procedure. So how do you boot the computer in order to run a virus scan to repair the boot sector? It's a classic chicken-and-egg situation — how do you do it?

You may need to boot your computer using the antivirus program's rescue disk, which may be a CD-ROM or a floppy disk. With some antivirus programs, the CD-ROM you installed the program from *is* the rescue disk. In other cases, you'll have to build the rescue disk yourself — *in advance* of your catastrophe. Hindsight isn't much help in a situation like this, so it's best to create the rescue disk when you first install your antivirus program. I describe this important step in Chapter 4.

Every antivirus program is different in terms of how their rescue disk works. Some will start up and immediately go to work, scanning and repairing the hard drive's master boot record, eliminating it of any virus-induced problems. Others will ask you what you want to do. Think "scan and fix."

If the rescue disk doesn't find anything wrong, then chances are that it's not a virus that's keeping your computer from booting, but some other problem. Time to find your copy of *Windows For Dummies* or *Troubleshooting Your PC For Dummies,* or find your expert friend's phone number.

Restoring files from backup

If a virus has trashed one of your files, your antivirus program may have had no choice but to remove the file if it was unable to repair it. If this has occurred, you have little choice but to restore the file(s) from your backups.

Don't have backups? Sit down; I have to tell you something: If the virus that infected your computer deleted one or more of your files, and you don't have copies of those files elsewhere, they may be irretrievably gone. But you still may have a glimmer of hope. The remainder of this section provides places where copies of the file may exist, and if that doesn't work, check out the following section, "Using a file-recovery utility."

This is an amazingly bad time to tell you that you "should have" been doing backups of some kind all along. *Windows* certainly doesn't tell you, and maybe nobody else did (well, shame on them). I'm sorry. But don't lose hope yet. There is a remote possibility that a copy of your missing file(s) can be found somewhere. I'll explain with an example.

Let's say a virus removed your file `resume.doc`. There are some places you can look to find either a copy of that file, or an older version of it. Here are some ideas:

> ✔ If your word-processing program is configured to create backup files, then maybe a backup of your file is still around. Depending on your word-processing program, a

backup copy of `resume.doc` may be called `resume.bak`, `Backup of resume.doc` (see Figure 7-4), or something else. Dig into the documentation of your word-processing program and see what its specific approach is.

✔ When you edit or use files, sometimes a word-processing program (as well as other types of programs) creates temporary files that may contain part (or even all) of the content you hated to lose. The names of these temporary files vary, and depend on the program that you use. Where these files can be found also varies. But I'd suggest you look for files whose names begin with a tilde (~), as well as files whose names end in `.tmp`. There may be other names, too.

✔ Did you e-mail any of the lost files to someone else? If so, then you have two options: The person or persons you mailed the files to may still have them and can mail them back, or, your e-mail program may have a "Sent Items" folder (which would contain a copy of mail messages you sent to other persons and, if you sent attachments to those persons, usually the attached files would be there too).

Two backup files

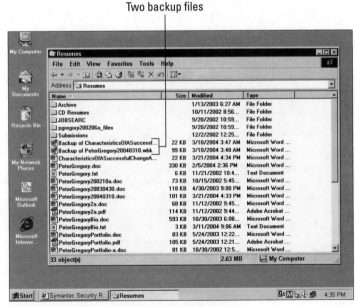

Figure 7-4: A listing of documents and backup files.

Using a file-recovery utility

It may be possible to recover a file damaged by a virus with one of several file-recovery utility programs. These programs scan your hard drive, looking for traces of files that may have been removed by a virus.

Some of these utilities work best if you install them *before* damage occurs. But depending upon the type of damage the virus incurred, it's still possible that a deleted file can be recovered after the damage is done.

I'm not an I-told-you-so kind of person, but in terms of file recovery due to viruses, file recovery utilities are all but unnecessary if basic safeguards are taken to protect your computer. However, if the horse is out of barn — as it were — then such a utility may be of help.

Some of the available file recovery utilities include:

- ✔ **File Rescue Plus:** Recovers deleted and corrupted files from many types of media. Available from `www.file-rescue.com`.

- ✔ **Aid System Restorer:** Made for Windows 95, Windows 98, and Windows ME, this is a backup-and-restore program that must be used prior to a virus damaging a computer's data. Available from `www.aidsoft.com/asr`.

- ✔ **Undelete 4.0:** This utility can be used to recover files that have been deleted from a Windows system. It can't be used to recover corrupted files. Undelete is available from `www.execsoft.com/undelete`.

If you're able to recover a corrupted program using one of these utilities, I still recommend that you consider this recovery temporary, while you obtain a "genuine" copy of the program from the software manufacturer or the release media, such as the CD.

If the file or files you lost are of great economic importance, you may be able to find an expert disk-recovery company that can use advanced techniques to attempt to find your lost files. This is potentially expensive (hundreds of dollars or more), but possibly worth it to you, if no other options work out.

Removing a Registry key

It's possible that the instructions you receive from a virus-removal tool or from a support technician may tell you to edit your Registry database. The Registry is a special database in the computer that contains a multitude (literally thousands) of configuration settings used by Windows and many of the programs installed on the computer.

Many viruses make changes to the computer's Registry, and occasionally, it's necessary to manually remove a Registry key in order to completely eliminate the effects of a virus infection. This section provides you with instructions for deleting a key or entire branch of the Registry.

Edit the Registry with extreme care, and *only* edit the Registry when virus-removal instructions or a support technician tells you to do so. If you make a mistake, you can *literally* break your computer so that it will not function correctly or possibly render your computer unbootable.

To remove a Registry key, follow these steps:

1. **Close all of the programs running on your computer.**

   If you're in the middle of a virus search-and-destroy mission, you shouldn't have any program running except those you need for repairs.

2. **Choose Start⇨Run.**

   The Run dialog box appears.

3. **Type** regedt32 **and then press Enter. (If regedt32 can't be found, then type** regedit **and then press Enter.)**

   The Registry Editor program starts. It looks a lot like Windows Explorer, including the presence of the Registry hierarchy that looks a lot like the directories-and-files hierarchy on your hard drive.

4. **Very, *very* carefully, navigate into the Registry to locate the Registry key in question (as directed by the virus-removal instructions).**

   For instance, if you're looking for the key *HKEY_LOCAL_MACHINE/ SOFTWARE/Microsoft/Command Processor/AutoRun,* then you can either double-click each entry or press the little plus symbol (as shown to the left of this paragraph) next to each entry, starting with HKEY_LOCAL_MACHINE, then SOFTWARE, and so on, to open each successive branch of the tree until you reach the destination.

5. **Make the required deletion, as follows:**

- If you must delete a branch (or folder) from the registry, select (click on) the branch to remove it, then press the Delete key. You'll need to confirm that this is the correct part to delete (see Figure 7-5).

  Check, double-check, and triple-check that you're deleting the correct branch! This is *very* dangerous territory!

- If you must delete a key (or value) from the Registry, then navigate to the branch in the registry containing the key. The keys in the branch will be listed on the right side of the window. Click on the key that you're directed to remove and press the Delete key. You'll need to verify your deletion. Do so carefully!

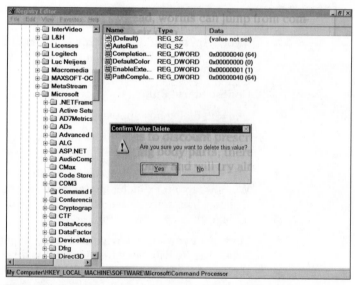

Figure 7-5: Repairing the Registry with the Registry Editor program.

6. **Exit the Registry editor.**

> You can now resume with the instructions furnished with the virus-removal instructions. It's usually a good idea to restart the computer after changing the registry, as many changes do not take effect until restarting the computer.

Reinstalling software

Sure, it's possible to repair the damaged software, but repairing it may be so difficult that it would just be easier to reinstall it. This is similar to an automobile accident, where you discover that the cost to repair the damage to a vehicle exceeds its value.

The information you get from your antivirus maker is usually what clinches a decision to reinstall software. For instance, they may tell you that a particular virus is known to severely damage Outlook Express and that you're better off removing and reinstalling the program. Why could this be? Behold:

- The repair procedure, even when performed by a program, can be complicated.

- The virus may damage different computers in different ways, making it difficult to write a repair program that works properly.

- The virus may remove important files that the program uses, making it necessary to reload those files from the original release media.

- There are more good reasons out there, but I'm close to deadline — I've got to get this chapter turned in to the publisher.

In such a situation, it's wise to keep good records on all the software programs you use on your computer — and here are some stellar examples:

- **Hang on to that original documentation.** This is especially important when you're required to type in a license key number to activate your program after you install it.

- **Keep track of the installation options chosen when you originally installed the program.** You may want to use the same ones.

✓ **Know where your original distribution medium is.**
Where *did* you put that CD-ROM, floppy disk, or stone
tablet (just kidding)? In the event you purchased a product online, know where to retrieve it if you need to reload
it. (Come to think of it, did the online instructions have
you create a boot disk when you downloaded the program? Better go find it.)

While it may be elegant to keep all of your license keys on
your computer, if the information on your computer is damaged, then your license keys are gone, too. You should either
write down the license keys in the product manual, on the
media case, directly on the CD, or in a binder containing information about your PC. If you cannot find the license key, you
will need to call the software company's customer support
department and plead your case with them. You'll find more
great ideas in Chapter 12.

Reinstalling Windows

Sometimes a virus is so destructive that there is little, if any,
hope of being able to repair the damage done to your
Windows operating system. This is about the most extreme
measure that someone would have to take in order to get his
or her computer back into proper running condition.

Depending on the damage that was done, and on the version
of Windows that you are using, there is a possibility that you
will lose *all* of your data files.

Reinstalling Windows is a step that cannot be taken lightly.
(Hint: Are you doing anything — *else* — this weekend?) I
would compare it to a situation where termites may have
done so much damage to your home that the only remedy
would be to tear it down — with the added possibility that
you may lose part or all of the contents of your home.

Part III

Maintaining Your Vigilance

The 5th Wave   By Rich Tennant

@RICHTENNANT.COM

"We're here to sweep for viruses."

In this part . . .

*I*t's very important to keep the signature file up to date in order to defend yourself against the latest viruses. If your memory is like mine, you should set your antivirus program to automatically get signature file updates.

A security patch is a package that is used to repair a flaw in software. Some flaws create security vulnerabilities that make it possible for someone (or some *thing*) to make bad things happen to your computer. It's not difficult to install security patches, but there are certain precautions that are necessary in order to keep your data safe.

Besides antivirus programs, two other types of security software can help protect your computer: firewalls and antispyware programs. Firewalls block scans and intrusion attempts from hackers and Internet worms. Antispyware programs block and/or remove software components that track your movements on the Internet — and worse.

If you use a PDA, you should consider using antivirus software on your PDA too. While the number of viruses that have been created to attack PDAs is low, certainly more PDA attacks will develop over time.

There are many good practices that you will want to consider in order to keep your computer and information safe. From backups to safe browser settings to blocking spyware, these factors will help to ensure that you and your computer will be safe.

Chapter 8

Updating Antivirus Software and Signatures

*S*ignature updates are the lifeblood of your antivirus program. Without them, your antivirus program can become (in effect) obsolete in less than a month. Any of the newest viruses can penetrate your computer if your virus signatures are (you guessed it) not up to date.

In this chapter, I describe the process of obtaining an updated signature file for your antivirus software, and I give you some hints about how often you may want to do so.

Getting a Signature Update

In order to detect and remove viruses, your antivirus program needs to know how to recognize them. Antivirus programs keep a *signature file* close by — a collection of virus descriptions that works like a dictionary and lists every known virus. When your antivirus program is doing its job — whether keeping a close eye on the programs and files your computer is using, or scanning the entire hard drive — it constantly compares the files it's looking at with all known virus signatures. If it finds a match, then the antivirus program has detected a virus.

Onslaught of the new viruses

Sounds like a horror movie, doesn't it? Bingo. New viruses are coming out all the time — over 20 each day, on average. And the new viruses are usually the ones that are spreading from computer to computer. Old viruses are seldom seen unless somebody comes up with a nasty new modification — in which case, your antivirus program will need an updated signature for the new virus (called a "variant") so it knows exactly what to look for.

What this means is that your antivirus program needs to periodically get a new copy of the signature file. The new copy of the signature file will contain all the virus signatures that were there before, along with the new signatures for all those new viruses.

Updates (had better) happen

A *signature update* is the task your antivirus program does to get a new, up-to-date signature file. The antivirus program attempts to establish a connection over the Internet to the antivirus company that made it. If it can make a connection, the antivirus program asks whether there's a newer version of the signature file. It's the equivalent of asking, "I have a signature file that is Version 4.16 — do you have anything newer than that?" If the company's Web site has a newer version, then the antivirus program copies it onto your computer.

Engine updates, too

Many antivirus programs can also update their engines. Sorry, no chrome exhaust pipes or higher gas mileage here — the *engine* is the part of the program that actually performs a specific, required task (in this case, the *detection engine* detecting viruses). The engine contains the instructions that tell the antivirus program which files to examine and what to look for. Occasionally, when some new type of virus is released, the antivirus company realizes it must make some adjustments on *how* the program looks for and detects viruses. So, as with signature files, the detection engines will also have version numbers, and your antivirus program can also download a new engine if a newer one is available. It's a constant game of catch-up with the virus writers who think of new ways to transmit and hide viruses.

People who work with antivirus software toss around different terms to describe this update process. Some call it a virus update, signature update, virus signature update, engine update, or just an update. And your particular brand of antivirus software may have a fancy name for it. Symantec calls theirs LiveUpdate, McAfee calls it SecurityCenter Update, and Panda uses the term Intelligent Update.

What version do I have?

It's usually fairly easy to see what version of signatures, engine, and possibly other antivirus components you have on your computer. Each brand of antivirus program is a little different, but usually Help➪About (or a similar command) will show you the version numbers and other pertinent information (as shown in Figure 8-1).

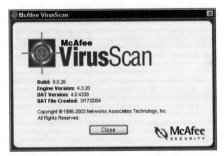

Figure 8-1: Antivirus software can display the versions of its signature file and other components.

It will occasionally be important to know what version of signatures you have on your computer. You may learn of a new virus outbreak and be concerned about whether you're protected. Here's a typical scenario that plays out every day somewhere in the world. . . .

How it goes (example scenario)

Suppose you learn about a new virus outbreak — a beastie called (say) W32.Dummy.A is ravaging the Web, and you have a particular concern about it (for example, friends or colleagues have found it lurking on their computers). Typically, your course of action looks like this:

1. **You visit your antivirus program's Web site to read about the new virus and what to do about it.**

   You immediately find exactly what you're looking for (what the heck, may as well be optimistic): The virus is indeed new and its awful habits are described on the Web site. You find a link with its name, and one click later, you're mulling over some specific information about the virus — the "R-rated" gory details describing how it gets around and what it does to victim computers.

2. **You locate the latest signature file.**

   All antivirus companies tell you the "minimum" version of signature file you must have in order to detect and stop the virus from infecting your computer. So you click the name of this particular virus and find where it says what signature file is required (say, Version 5.26.079).

3. **You check to see which version of the signature file you now have.**

   Usually that means consulting your antivirus program's help files (Help⇨About) in your antivirus program while it's running. Say you find that you have 5.26.077 — a couple of numbers behind the minimum (5.26.079). Better download that later version of the signature file.

4. **You tell your antivirus program to update the signature file.**

   With your antivirus program running, you select the Update Now (or equivalent) function. Your program immediately downloads the latest signature file from the antivirus company's Web site, and tells you when the new signature file is downloaded and successfully installed.

5. **You check to make sure the new signature file fills the bill.**

Virus signatures as mug shots and fingerprints

Technically speaking, of course, a virus contains programming instructions that the virus needs in order to work. The instructions have to be transferred with the virus or it can't function. But those instructions also form a distinctive pattern that identifies the virus as effectively as a fingerprint identifies a human. Comparing viruses to criminals is especially apt, so here's a crime story....

Imagine your computer as a large office building with a security guard (your antivirus program) watching its entrance: People come in off the streets of Internet City, some legit, some not so legit. The security guard looks at the face of each person coming in and compares it to the photographs of known criminals on file. If someone's face matches that of a known criminal, that person is not permitted to enter the building. Sometimes criminals walk in wearing bad disguises, but the guard is prepared: The file includes mug shots *and* fingerprints. Whoever walks up and asks to be let in gets a fingerprint check as standard operating procedure. Bad guys get thrown in the cooler.

To stay effective, the guard updates his known-criminals file every day. New criminals are betting that their pictures aren't in the file yet. But the fingerprints — the virus signatures — will finger 'em every time.

Another quick Help⇨About command shows that you now have version 5.26.080 — one release *newer* than 5.26.079. You're protected, all right.

6. **Wary that you may already have the virus as a nasty guest, you scan your entire computer for viruses.**

    Now that you have that newest signature file on your computer, you can be sure that if W32.Dummy.A is skulking around on your computer, your antivirus program will find it — and, if possible, remove it and repair the infected file. If the virus isn't found, then you're clean and protected from the current version. (Gotta love those win-win situations.)

The process rarely gets more complicated than this.

Deciding How Often to Get Updates

Some questions crop up often — "Does my computer have a virus?" "How do I scan for a virus?" "Does Dick Clark wear a toupee?" — but the most-often-asked question about antivirus programs is, "How often should I get updates?"

If I was more of a blarney artist, I would attempt to impress you (or bore you) with statistics that would tell you precisely how often to update your virus-signature files. Instead, I'll provide a shortcut, a simple answer that lays out some practical approaches and why it's reasonable to use them:

- **Always-on, broadband Internet connection:** If your computer is connected to the Internet all the time, update your signature files at least once or twice each day. If you work with sensitive data that you can't afford to lose, updating up to *six* times a day would be better. On a slow news day, this might be construed as overkill, and any more than six times a day *would* be overkill. But sometimes a really nasty virus is on the loose and multiple variants are popping up every day. If you have to continue your work on a day like this, hunker down and update your signatures every hour or two until the crisis passes.

- **Dial-up Internet connection:** You can update less frequently because your computer isn't such an attractive target to viruses. Generally you're at lower risk of infection because an always-on connection (which generally requires lots of bandwidth) isn't practical for dial-up use. With normal dial-up, you're offline (and unavailable to viruses) much of the time, so updating once (or sometimes twice) a week is fine . If you update virus signatures more often over a dial-up connection (say, once or twice daily), it could add to your monthly connect charges.

- **On-the-edge computer habits:** If you're a wee bit paranoid, or if your computing habits are high-risk, then you *could* try to update as often as once each hour. Antivirus makers don't charge extra for obsessive updating, but consider this: Is their latest update likely to change *that* fast? Would it be simpler to change your habits?

Getting Updates

Signature updates are your antivirus program's ammunition. Without regular signature updates, your antivirus program quickly becomes dependent on unreliable ammo — which is to say, practically useless. Fortunately, getting the good new stuff is pretty straightforward, whether you do it manually or automatically.

Manual updates

Antivirus programs permit you to do signature file updates "on demand" — in other words, anytime you want. If, unlike me, you have a terrific memory, then you can just remember to do signature file updates as often as needed.

Every antivirus program is designed a little differently: Each has a manual signature-updating capability, but each has a different way of "navigating" to it. In some programs, you can click the antivirus icon in the system tray and see a Download Signature Now command right next to the system tray. (Figure 8-2 shows what a typical Trend Micro manual download looks like.) Other programs require you to open the antivirus program first, click the appropriate tab, and *then* download virus signatures.

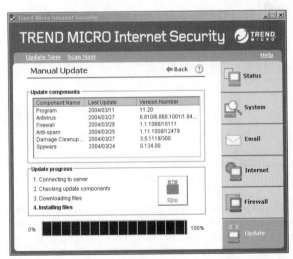

Figure 8-2: A manual download of virus signatures in progress.

Automatic updates

Most antivirus programs also let you schedule automatic updates that your computer can do as often as you like. Personally, I like this option: I may forget to update virus signatures, but my computer will never forget to.

Telling your antivirus program how often to update your signature files is easier than programming your VCR (see Figure 8-3 for a typical example). Finding the screen to set this up is another matter, but generally antivirus programs are not all that complicated, so hopefully you can find it quickly. You can read the manual, look at help, or visit the Web site to see how it's done.

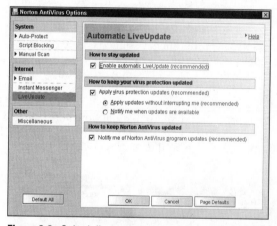

Figure 8-3: Scheduling automatic updates — hey, no blinking 12:00! Cool!

One note about automatic updates: Your computer must be running, and it must be either connected to the Internet or able to automatically connect to the Internet when the update takes place. If you have any doubt at all whether an automatic update will work, schedule one to take place five minutes from now and watch what happens.

Even when you think your virus-signature updates will be successful most of the time, I still think it's a good idea to look at the version numbers of your virus-signature files to make sure those updates are really happening. If your automatic updates are constantly failing, you'll quickly be in a position of vulnerability to new viruses. Going more than a week without virus-signature updates is a bad state to be in.

If your updates aren't happening, check your automatic-update configuration to see if it's *really* enabled (did you set the schedule but fail to activate it?). You can also try a manual update — if that works, then you have a scheduling problem. If it doesn't work, then the update process itself is failing. Visit your antivirus program's Web site and look for the Help, Support, or FAQ section so that you can figure out why updates aren't working.

Scanning after an Update

If suddenly the realization hits that it's been more than a week since you updated your virus-signature file, you better scan your computer for viruses immediately — particularly if you're the active type (lots of e-mail, file sharing, file swapping, opening mail from strangers, and other such cyber-exuberance).

The more time that has gone by since your last signature update, the more important it is that you do a whole-system scan. For instance, if two weeks has elapsed since your last update, then any virus less than two weeks old could have entered your computer unhindered. Here's why that's a cause for concern:

- The viruses you're likeliest to catch are new; your antivirus software doesn't yet know how to detect them.

- New viruses are joining the online feeding frenzy every day. If you haven't update your defenses for two weeks, who knows how many viruses looked at your computer, went *yum, yum,* and moved right in?

Go to Chapter 6 for more information on how to perform manual scans, and how to set up your antivirus program to perform regularly scheduled scans automatically while you sleep. And don't be surprised if you sleep better.

Chapter 9

Installing Security Patches

● ●

● ●

*B*esides running antivirus software and firewall software, installing security patches is one of the most important ways you can make your computer more secure. Although not yet as simple as running antivirus software, installing security patches isn't difficult when you get the hang of it.

In this chapter, you get a handle on what security patches are, why they're needed, and the different ways to install them.

Figuring Out Why You Need Security Patches

The big software programs that run on PCs today consist of thousands — and sometimes even millions — of lines of *source code* (the step-by-step instructions that give the program its functionality and personality). That's a lot to keep track of — and (as with anything made by people) flaws can creep in.

Software can be as complex as any mechanical orchestration of gears, shafts, pulleys, bearings, levers, switches, and so on. But unlike physical machinery, software is almost entirely abstract — it's a set of electronic instructions. You can't just hold it in your hand or put a wrench on it to tighten it up; that makes it harder to examine for strength, robustness, resiliency, and integrity.

It's difficult to watch software's inner workings in action: There is rarely something you can actually watch. Even a word-processing program consists of mostly mathematical calculations, data buffers, table lookups, device management, and other steps that mostly push electrons around, far removed from what we see on the screen.

Challenges like this make it difficult to know whether a complex software program is error-free and whether it does *exactly* what it's supposed to do — *and nothing else.*

The problem of ensuring that a single software program is error-free is compounded by the way that computers and networks interact today. Within a single computer, there may be dozens of different programs all running at once, talking with each other on a variety of topics.

Such internal conversations take place thousands of times each second. When you visit a Web site, you bring in thousands of HTML, JavaScript, ActiveX, Shockwave, and Acrobat computer instructions in nearly infinite combinations, subjecting the software in your computer to situations that no one ever anticipated — not the specification people, the designers, the software engineers, or the testers.

But there are some people who work day and night looking for such obscure situations. Their very existence is driven by the need to find flaws, especially those that can be exploited. (You can read more about this in Chapter 13.)

Addressing vulnerabilities

Errors can make software programs function in ways other than those the makers intended. Even so, many errors in common programs (such as word processors) aren't even observable. They happen somewhere inside the program, where they're sometimes hard to detect. Those that are observable are commonly called "bugs."

There is one type of bug in a software program that is called a *vulnerability*. The word *vulnerability* implies some type of a weakness. When a *person* is vulnerable, he or she can be hurt more easily. Likewise, a vulnerability — also known as a *security flaw* or *security hole* — means a program is (in effect) gullible; certain conditions or instructions can make it perform some function that it should not be *allowed* to do. This would be kind like the not-so-diligent security guard who stops watching the building's entrance when a certain pretty woman walks in and starts sweet-talking him, permitting the crooks with the loot to stroll right by unnoticed.

Serious vulnerabilities permit a program to perform functions that corrupt or damage software or information on the computer. Now and then, some vulnerabilities are so critical that they are easily exploited by persons with advanced knowledge and ill intent. The result? Reprehensible: the release of damaging viruses, Trojan horses, and Internet worms, causing banks to close, airlines to cancel flights, and e-voting machines to elect robots to public office (okay, so maybe not *all* vulnerabilities are bad).

The term "bug" first got its name in the 1940s when computers contained thousands of electromechanical relays. A malfunction in a computer was once traced to a moth that had flown into a relay and caused it to stop working. Ever since, computer malfunctions have been called bugs, after that first moth. What would we have called malfunctions if the first one was traced to a kernel of popcorn or a paper clip?

Closing the holes

A natural response to the threat of viruses is to fix the vulnerabilities. When a software company such as Microsoft discovers a vulnerability in one of its software programs, the response is to devise some sort of change to the program. The change must permit the program to continue functioning correctly, but eliminate the vulnerability. Not always easy.

When a vulnerability is discovered, the software company assigns the task of designing a *patch* to one or more junior programmers (think I'm kidding?) — a patch is nothing more than a correctly rewritten part of the existing computer program. The assignment is to change a bit of the flawed program in a way that — with any luck — permits it to retain all its intended functionality, eliminating only the security hole.

Why are they called patches?

The computer software industry has borrowed (or, should I say, lifted) a number of terms from the English language to describe things in the world of computers and software — *virus, Trojan horse, worm,* and *patch.* Sure, *patch* may sound a little shabby, suggesting a tire or inflatable beach toy with a piece of material stuck over a small hole to prevent air from escaping. But that's how it works. A patch is a quick fix that covers a "hole" in the code by providing some lines of improved code; it doesn't revise the whole program. It just keeps the data from leaking out too fast.

Specific patches exist for specific problems. A *security patch* is used to close a security hole — some vulnerability that permits an undesirable function or behavior.

A complicated computer program (say, a Web browser or word processor) may have thousands of separate components, packaged into dozens — even hundreds — of separate files. Any patch that a software company creates is just a corrected version of one or more of these files. It's a little bit like changing one light bulb on a holiday display that contains hundreds or thousands of lights — without accidentally causing any of the other lights to stop working.

Simplifying updates

To simplify the patching procedure, the software companies rarely just make a newer version of a program file, but instead they package the corrected program file within another program that installs the patch for you. So rather than having to wade through instructions that tell you (among other things) to replace the file `winnt/system32/dcom3.dll` dated February 3, 2004, with the file by the same name dated April 4, 2004, all you need to do is double-click the installer program. (Whew! That was a close one.)

The installer program can also do a lot of checking and testing. Most patches only work with one particular version of a program, so the installer program must perform some other checks:

✔ It checks the version of the program being patched.

✔ It checks to see whether the patch has already been installed.

✔ It determines whether there's enough disk space on the computer for the patch to be installed without causing errors.

✔ It creates some log-file entries to document when this patch was installed on the computer.

✔ It creates entries in a special "uninstall" directory for later use if you decide to remove the patch.

Scrutinizing Security Patches

Before you go grab and install a security patch, you may want to get to know a few basic facts about it — where to get it, what it does, whether it'll cost you, that sort of thing. Most software makers have this process figured out, more or less, even if they don't collectively take what I'd call a consistent approach to the matter.

Some software programs periodically "call home" to see whether patches are available for them. They'll even download and install their own updates if you let them. Other software makers are kind enough to send you e-mail if they release a new security patch. Some offer mailing lists that inform members automatically about new developments (including security patches) via e-mail. Other software makers make you find — and periodically visit — the company Web site to check for any new patches.

And then you have the clueless software makers who don't seem to know what patches are. Fortunately, they're the minority. If you're using software made by the rest (those who understand the need for patches and act accordingly), here's a general rundown on security patches from some of the major software companies.

A few companies don't publicize their patches at all, but wait until you call with a specific problem addressed by their (ahem) secret patch. Fortunately, few companies do that anymore. It's better for business to just fess up to one's mistakes and show customers where to find the fixes.

The Microsoft Security page

When it comes to notifying users about critical security patches, Microsoft is very well organized (they get lots of practice), and you have a number of options available to you. They have a nice Web page dedicated to the latest security information about their products — and a mailing list you can join that lets you know the minute any new security patches are available. You have two ways to get the goods:

✔ To see the Microsoft Security Web site, go to `www.microsoft.com/security`. There you'll find a great number of features and information.

✔ To get on Microsoft's mailing list for critical patches, go to their Security Web page and click the <u>Get e-mail about new security updates</u> link. You'll be taken to a sign-up screen where you put in your e-mail address. From that point forward, you're notified via e-mail whenever any critical situation is going on.

My personal preference is to keep all bases covered. I subscribe to the mailing list, but I still periodically visit the Microsoft Security Web page to see what's new.

Except on rare occasions, Microsoft releases security patches once a month — on the second Tuesday — as part of their grand plan. Consumers normally don't pay much attention, but for large companies — with tens of thousands of computers running Windows — it matters a great deal. Knowing that patches come out on a predictable schedule permits large companies to organize security upgrades. From my own experience in large companies, such predictability is greatly preferable to the near-chaos that occurred back in the Dark Ages when Microsoft used to "shotgun" their security patches with little or no advance notice.

Non-Microsoft programs

Companies other than Microsoft use a variety of methods to inform their customers about available security patches (such as mailing lists and Web sites). Some companies have figured out that viruses are bad for *all* Internet business, and go beyond simply offering patches for their own products. Most of the antivirus companies offer downloadable fixes for specific viruses — to everybody, even the folks who aren't using their software. (Are they altruistic? Are they nuts? Nope, just smart.)

Other sources of security information

A couple of other high-quality sources of security information are well worth a look — and I recommend you consider viewing them on a regular basis (or, easier yet, getting on their mailing lists). Some of the better ones include these:

- ✔ **US-CERT.** The United States Computer Emergency Readiness Team manages the National Cyber Alert System. You can subscribe to security alerts written for non-computer experts (which includes most people on the planet). Go to `www.us-cert.gov` to view cybersecurity tips and sign up for the bulletins.

- ✔ **AusCERT.** This is the Australian Computer Emergency Response Team. Yes, they get viruses down under too. You can view alerts and subscribe to their mailing list. Go to `www.auscert.org` for more information.

Preparing to Install Security Patches

Software is pretty complicated — it's a multitude of modules contained in dozens or hundreds of separate computer files. A patch installation involves replacing one or more of these files, and perhaps tinkering with other parts of the software, which makes the process (you guessed it) complex. Therefore, in the name of sanity, I suggest you do the following before you install any security patches:

1. **Back up your important files.**

   If you're not sure what this means or how to do a backup, go to Chapter 12.

2. **Restart your computer.**

   Rebooting is a good idea before installing any patches. A freshly booted operating system is more stable. Things will just go better.

3. **Find and carefully read the installation instructions associated with the patch.**

   Usually there is additional information that discusses any known side effects or situations you may need to know about. It's best if you're aware of these before you install the patch, especially because a few patches cannot be removed after they have been installed.

 It's a good idea to install one patch at a time, reboot after each patch installation, and run your computer for a while to make sure it's running okay before you install the next patch. Call me cautious, but I've not had a significant problem in many years with installations I've done after following these principles.

If your computer is running low on system resources — whether that's processor speed, amount of memory, or available disk space — you may experience a dramatic slowdown after installing a patch or upgrade. If this happens to you, that last patch may have been the straw that broke the camel's back. What can you do?

Well, you can try and back out the patch, but that may or may not help. The action of installing the patch may have contributed to the "entropy" of your computer by moving system files around on the disk (for example) in a way that won't be undone if you remove the patch. Everyone's needs are different: You may need a faster processor, more memory, a larger or faster disk, or any combination of these.

Installing Security Patches

This is where the rubber meets the road. You know you need to check for and install security patches. You are *prepared* to install them (right?), and you're ready to start. This section shows you how.

Downloading from Windows Update

Microsoft has generously provided a Web page where you can allow their computer to examine your computer to determine what available patches are missing from your computer. It's really quite a nice setup.

To use Windows Update, you need an Internet connection and Windows Internet Explorer Version 5 or newer. Sorry, you Netscape, Mozilla, and Opera users — you must use IE to use Windows Update. Microsoft is just funny that way.

Follow this procedure to obtain patches using Windows Update:

1. **Follow the steps I describe in the section titled "Preparing to Install Security Patches," earlier in this chapter.**

2. **Point your browser to the following site:**

   `http://windowsupdate.microsoft.com`

3. **Click the <u>Scan for updates</u> link, as shown in Figure 9-1.**

Click here to scan for new patches.

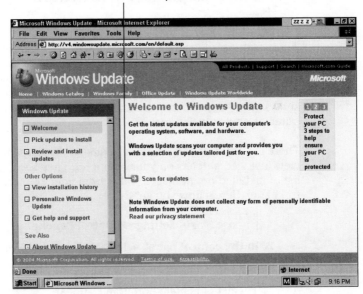

Figure 9-1: The Windows Update start page.

Microsoft analyzes your computer, looks at the versions of your operating system and tools, and compares its findings against a list of all available patches for your computer. No personal information will be sent from your computer to Microsoft, and the plastic bag will not inflate.

4. **If there are patches to install, click the <u>Review and install updates</u> link and then the <u>Critical Updates and Service Packs</u> link.**

   You see all of the critical patches and updates that are needed for your computer.

5. **Review the selected patches.**

   You can read more about each one by clicking the <u>Read more</u> link. Remove any that you don't want (you should install all of them); then click the Install Now button, as shown in Figure 9-2.

   A dialog box appears, listing patches that are being installed.

6. **Sometimes you see an End User License Agreement. After reading it (frankly, I rarely do), click Accept.**

   The patch-installation process begins.

Another thing you can do with Windows Update is see what patches are already installed on your computer. To view installed patches, go to the Windows Update Web page and click the <u>View installation history</u> link in the left column. It shows you which patches are already installed on your computer, as shown in Figure 9-3.

There is a third way (good things come in threes, right?) to view installed patches on your computer. They show up on a list of installed programs, viewable from your computer's control panel. Here's how you get there:

1. **Choose Start⇨Settings⇨Control Panel.**

2. **In the control panel, select Add/Remove Programs.**

   Figure 9-4 shows what you get on-screen.

   The list of installed programs appears.

3. **Scroll down to the bottom of the installed programs list.**

   Installed patches appear with the name Windows 2000 Hotfix or Windows XP Hotfix.

Click here to install.

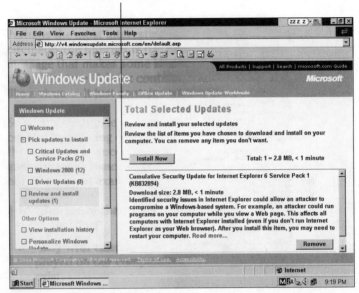

Figure 9-2: Windows Update shows which updates need to be installed.

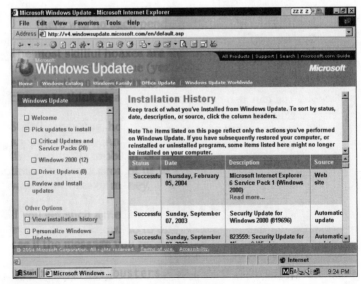

Figure 9-3: The patches installed on this computer.

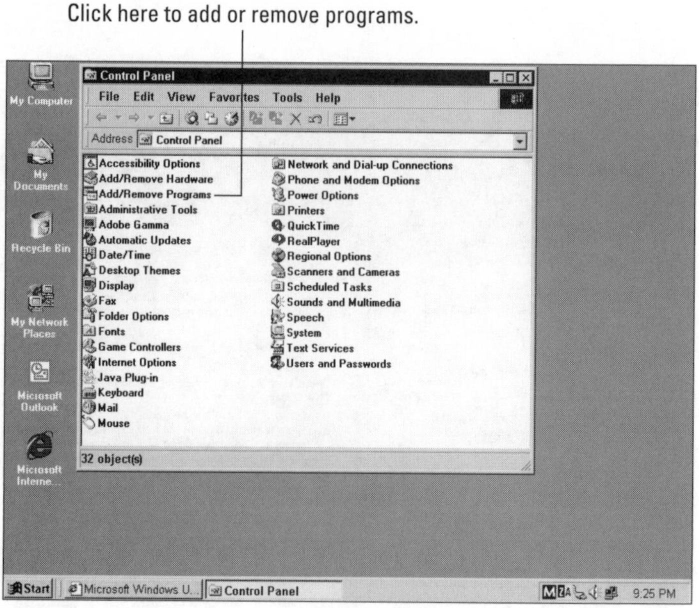

Click here to add or remove programs.

Figure 9-4: Windows control panel, with Add/Remove Programs indicated.

Patches are referenced by KB (Knowledge Base) article number. It's easy to figure out what this is — you can go to www.microsoft.com and type in the KB article number on Microsoft's home page (as shown in Figure 9-5), which takes you to the article that describes the patch.

You can also go to support.microsoft.com and click on the Knowledge Base Article ID Number Search link near the top of the page. Either way, you're able to quickly get to detailed (sometimes *too* detailed!) information about any patch.

They don't just aim at Windows

Patches for Microsoft Office are just as vital as those for Microsoft Windows itself. This is because Microsoft Office includes Outlook, the popular e-mail program. Unpatched weaknesses in Outlook — in any of its various versions (such as the downloadable Outlook Express) — can let in an e-mail message containing malicious code. Result: Havoc on your computer. One lapse in security can ruin your whole day.

Article number to search for

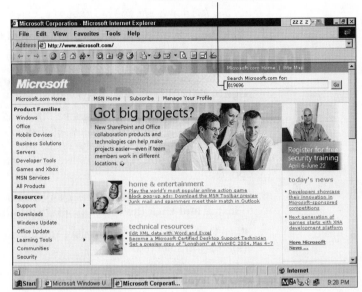

Figure 9-5: From the Microsoft home page, you can search for Knowledge Base articles.

Later in this chapter I show you how to get your computer to automatically download security updates.

Getting Office patches from Microsoft Office Update

If you're running Microsoft Office, then you need to periodically check on whether any security patches are needed. Microsoft Office programs have their fair share of security issues, so it is important to stay current on Office patches too! Keep all of your defenses covered!

Follow the instructions here to run Microsoft Office Update:

1. **Close all applications running on your computer (except for a Web browser).**

   A fresh reboot would be a good idea, too.

2. **Go to the Windows Update Web page at**

   `http://windowsupdate.microsoft.com`

3. **Click the Office Update link near the top of the page.**

   The Office Update screen (shown in Figure 9-6) appears.

4. **Click the <u>Check for Updates</u> link near the top of the page to start Microsoft's analysis of your computer.**

   The analyzer looks at the versions of the Microsoft Office program, comparing yours against a list of all available patches for Microsoft Office. After the analysis is complete, you see a list of available patches and updates.

5. **After reviewing the list, uncheck any you don't want to install and click the Start Installation button.**

   Office Update begins downloading and installing the updates you selected.

   You'll see an End-User License Agreement that you'll need to review (that's *before* you check with the legal department for a translation).

Click here to check for updates.

Figure 9-6: The Microsoft Office Update start screen.

Often, you will need your Microsoft Office CD handy when running Microsoft Office Update. In order to properly update Microsoft Office, the Update program needs to read information from your original CD.

Using Windows Automatic Update

In Windows 2000 and Windows XP, Microsoft has developed a nice feature in which a tiny program on your computer can automatically check for critical updates (and even automatically download them). A little pop-up window tells you that one or more critical security patches are available.

To see whether Automatic Updates is activated on your computer, open your computer's control panel (Choose Start⇨ Settings⇨Control Panel), and select Automatic Updates. If you don't see Automatic Updates on your control panel and you're running Windows XP, click Classic View and then you should see it.

If you still don't see Automatic Updates in your control panel, it's possible that it was not installed. Depending upon your skill and comfort level, you can either install it yourself, check with the store where you bought your computer, or give your expert friend or computer mentor a call.

In the Automatic Updates configuration window shown in Figure 9-7, you can see whether Automatic Updates is activated by seeing whether the Keep My Computer Up to Date check box is checked. If the check box is not checked and you would like to run Automatic Updates, check this box.

Then you need to select which of the three operating modes you want. You can select from one of the following:

- ✔ **Notify me before downloading any updates and notify me again before installing them on my computer.** This option is fine if you don't mind waiting for critical patches to download before they are installed.

- ✔ **Download updates automatically and notify me when they are ready to be installed.** This is my personal preference and a nice convenience feature: Your computer downloads the patches in advance, and all you have to do is install them.

✔ **Automatically download the updates and install them on the schedule that I specify.** I personally dislike this feature; I want more control over the installation of critical patches. But if this option suits your situation, then you choose the time of day and day of the week when you want critical patches automatically installed.

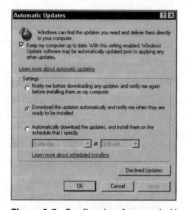

Figure 9-7: Configuring Automatic Updates.

When you're using your computer and Automatic Updates discovers that a critical patch is available for you to install, it will display a message near your system tray (as shown in Figure 9-8) saying that critical patches are available for installation on your computer (you won't see this message if you have configured Automatic Updates to automatically install patches for you).

There's also a do-it-yourself way to install critical patches using Automatic Update — coming right up. (In these examples, the option chosen was Download Updates Automatically.)

Automatic update system tray icon

Figure 9-8: Automatic updates announce their availability.

When you see the message that tells you updates are available, you can install the available updates by following these steps:

1. **Click anywhere on the balloon (except on the "X" if you're running Windows XP) to pull up the Automatic Updates dialog box.**

   You see a list of critical patches that need to be installed on your computer. Usually, all of them are already selected by default, and it's fine to leave them that way.

2. **If you're going to install patches, shut down all other programs.**

   It's likely that you'll need to reboot your computer right after the patches have been installed. If you have any critical files on your computer, it would be a good idea to back them up before you proceed.

   Usually it's fine to install all the patches at once. But if you are one of those "install one at a time" people like me, you can uncheck those that you wish to install later.

   If you're not ready to install these security patches now, you can defer the installation by clicking Remind Me Later — you can defer for up to three days. (I wouldn't advise doing this too many times; viruses keep emerging all the time. You should get those critical updates into your computer as soon as possible!)

3. **Click the Install button and your patch installation commences.**

After the critical patches have been installed, you may receive a message telling you that you need to reboot your computer. Because you already stopped all your other programs and backed up your files, you can (and should) reboot your computer as soon as you're asked to. If you must delay rebooting, please don't delay for too long (and don't install anything else in the meantime).

After you've got 'em, reboot to turn them on. Most critical patches aren't activated *until you reboot your computer.* Before then, they're installed but they're not yet running. A reboot is required so the computer knows they're in there; only then can they protect your computer from whatever bad stuff they're designed to prevent.

Should I run Automatic Updates?

You can configure Windows Automatic Updates to operate in one of three modes:

✔ **Notify Only:** In this mode, Automatic Updates periodically queries Microsoft to see whether any critical patches are available. If they are, you click "Install" to make Automatic Updates download and install them on your computer. I like this option — of course, it helps if you don't mind waiting for your computer to download the patches.

✔ **Download and Notify:** This is similar to Notify Only, except that Automatic Updates will download (but *not* install) all available critical patches. If any critical patches are available, you click Install and Automatic Updates installs the critical patches right away — you don't have to wait for a download to occur. One thing very nice about this feature

is that the download occurs while you're busy with other things, and you can install the patches even if you're offline because they are already on your computer. (This is my favorite option.)

✔ **Full Automatic:** In this option, Automatic Updates not only downloads critical patches from Microsoft, but also automatically installs all of them, at a time of day that you specify. This is a nice feature if you don't mind letting someone else decide which critical patches should be installed on your computer, without your permission. (Okay, allow me one grouse: If this was the only way that Automatic Updates worked, I wouldn't use it at all. I like to have some control over when critical patches are installed, and which ones.)

Downloading patches from the Microsoft Security Web site

The Security Web site at Microsoft (www.microsoft.com/security) has a great deal of information available for Microsoft customers, including specific information on the latest security patches that should be installed.

To install the latest security patches, click the <u>Install the Windows Security Update</u> link, which will take you to a page that lists the most recent security patches, along with a brief description and severity level (Low, Medium, High, Critical, The-Sky-Is-Falling). When you click on the link for each security patch, Microsoft takes you to the page for that particular patch, where download instructions and additional information are available.

Going to the Microsoft Security Web page is a good idea if you want to find a wide variety of security information. Advanced users can use this site to get detailed technical information about security patches (if you want an appreciation for the complexity of today's computer software, try reading one of them; just make sure you don't get your eyes stuck in the cross-eyed position). But the easiest way to get the patches and updates that your computer needs is through Windows Update (which I discuss a few pages back).

Downloading patches yourself

If you have a good level of experience with Windows, you can download your patches directly, without having to use Windows Update or Automatic Updates.

There is a wide variety of patches available for Microsoft products, and they tend to be scattered hither and yon throughout the Microsoft Web site, generally by topic. For instance, patches for Microsoft Office can be found on the Microsoft Office Web page, those for Windows on the Windows page, and so forth. You can also go to the general Downloads page and find patches there by searching for them by product name and version.

When you find a patch listed on a Web page, you can click on it to see more detail. See Figure 9-9.

To download and install a patch from the Microsoft Security Web site, follow this procedure:

1. **Select a patch to install from those listed as available for your computer.**

   Often you have to select the right patch; if you do not, flames will leap out of your computer's connectors and you'll be really sorry. Well, no, that's not quite true — but if you select a patch for some version of the software other than what you've installed, the patch will probably whine about a mismatch between the patch and the program it's intended to patch and refuse to continue.

2. Click on the link to download the patch.

The link may be the name of the file to download, or it may be the word *download*.

It's a good idea to choose Save, as this will save a copy of the patch locally on your computer. They're not all that big, and it's handy to have it locally in case you need to reinstall the patch, pass it to a friend who also needs it, or if you have a problem part-way through the installation.

3. Close all your other programs so that the only thing running is the patch installation itself.

You can even close your Web browser; you won't need it anymore for this procedure.

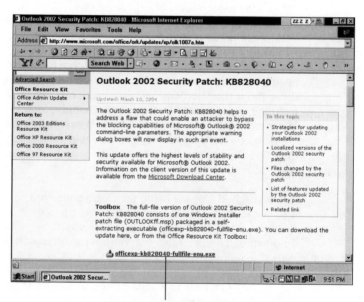

Click link to start download.

Figure 9-9: An Outlook Security patch about to be downloaded.

4. **Run the patch-installer program.**

   You can run the patch installer right from the Download dialog box by clicking Open after the download has completed, or find it with Windows Explorer and double-click it to run it that way.

   You see one or two dialog boxes that contain the usual disclaimers. After you get through those, the actual patch installation takes place.

5. **Reboot your computer.**

   Most of the time your computer asks for a reboot. I highly recommend that you do so, even if it doesn't ask you. You've already stopped all your other programs — right? — so this should be a minor inconvenience.

I think it's a good idea to reboot your computer after each security patch, in the event that you're installing more than one. I've been burned in the past by making too many changes without doing reboots in between them. I don't want the same thing to happen to you.

Patching other common programs

Once in a while, security patches are issued for non-Microsoft products. Like with Microsoft programs, vulnerabilities are occasionally discovered in these other programs that permit a wily hacker to break into your computer or damage your information. A few examples are listed here:

✔ **Adobe Acrobat Reader:** Nearly everyone has Acrobat Reader. Once in a while, a vulnerability is discovered in Adobe's PDF (Portable Document Format) language that necessitates a patch. Acrobat Reader is configured to automatically check for the availability of security patches. If a patch becomes available, you see a dialog box asking whether you wish to download and install an update.

✔ **RealAudio Player:** RealAudio Player is famous (or notorious, depending on your point of view) for staying in contact with the RealAudio company to keep you informed about new products. RealAudio Player displays a dialog box asking whether you want to update.

✔ **Macromedia Flash and Shockwave:** These programs are plug-ins to Internet Explorer (not separate programs), used to display certain animated graphics and other cool effects. These plug-ins are configured to "phone home" occasionally to see whether updates are available. Usually you see a terse dialog box that reads something like, "An update is available. Install now?" If you have a few minutes, these updates are generally a good idea to do.

✔ **Others:** Many other products have manual or automatic features to check for updates. You should become familiar with your programs and how to tell whether updates — particular security patches — are available. It's all a part of good computer hygiene.

The update you may be consenting to may or may not require a fee. Not all updates are free, and not all fee-based updates announce themselves clearly as such. And if you are using an old version of a software product, its manufacturer may no longer be creating updates or patches for it.

Installing Service Packs

A *service pack* is like a patch — it contains changes to software on your computer — but it's actually a *collection* of patches (as well as other changes) rolled into a major package and installed all at once.

Service packs can be found and installed using Windows Update, and you can also download them from the Microsoft Web site, but they're not available in Automatic Updates.

Microsoft creates service packs for Windows, Microsoft Office, Internet Explorer, and other products.

If you're diligent about security patches, then you'll want to know that quite often a service pack includes some security patches you've already installed on your computer. Don't worry — your computer knows what to do.

Generally I recommend installing service packs. My advice for your doing so comes with these conditions:

✓ **If you have an important deadline that you need to meet using your computer, finish your work first.** Service Pack installation takes a long time — and it can probably wait. In the meantime, to protect yourself, you can install the most critical individual security patches if you must.

✓ **Back up all your important files first (see Chapter 12).**

✓ **Reboot your computer after the service pack is installed.**

✓ **Read all available information about the service pack on Microsoft's Web site.** Because service packs often modify program features, it's a good idea to be familiar with what changes you can expect.

✓ **Give yourself plenty of time.** Service packs can take a very long time to download (as long as several hours), particularly if you have a dial-up connection.

✓ **Don't be too anxious to install a brand-new service pack.** Once in a great while, there is some problem associated with service packs. If you discover that a new service pack has been created, wait a week or two if you can. Any problems are usually identified and fixed in that period of time.

✓ **Make sure you have plenty of disk space.** Service packs in some cases require 10 MB, 20 MB, or even 50 MB of space. If your computer is really low on space, the service pack installation may fail (the service pack installation program checks available space, but I'm not so sure it's foolproof). But even if the service pack installation is successful, you don't want to be left with too little free space. This can make it hard for you to work with your files, and it's a known fact that a Windows computer with very little free space available (less than 5 percent) begins to get grumpy and slooooooooowwwwws down. Operating systems are fragile enough under ideal conditions, and it's not a good idea to stress them out.

To find the amount of free disk space in Windows 2000 and Windows XP, right-click on My Computer and select Explore.

> ✔ **After you install the service pack, reboot the computer and try things out to see if things work the same as before.**

The procedure for installing service packs is exactly the same as that for patches, whether you install them using Windows Update if you download them from the Microsoft Web site. Just be prepared for the installation to take quite a while.

Unlike patches, you must have your original CDs to complete the installation of a service pack for Microsoft Windows 2000, Windows XP, Microsoft Office 2000, Office XP, or Office 2003. If you can't find *your original CDs,* you won't be able to install the service pack!

Removing Patches

While it should be a rare occurrence, you may find yourself in a situation where you need to remove a patch. In the past several years, personally, I have never needed to remove a patch, but I was in a situation recently where an Internet Explorer (IE) patch changed the way that IE worked, in a very subtle but irritating way. But by the time I was ready to pull the patch out, Microsoft came out with a new security patch that fixed newly discovered vulnerabilities and (oh yeah) corrected the anomaly.

If you're not sure which patch you need to remove, you will need to cross-reference the "Q article" number found on Microsoft's Web site (Figure 9-10 shows an example). To find a specific Q article, type in Q and the article number (for example, Q324096) in the search field on Microsoft's Web site.

Read up on what the patch does before you try to remove it. Make sure the cure isn't worse than the disease. Then you can follow this procedure to remove the patch:

1. **Choose Start➪Settings➪Control Panel. Then select Add/Remove Programs.**

2. **If you're sure that you have identified a patch to remove, select it from the Add/Remove Programs window and click the Change/Remove button.**

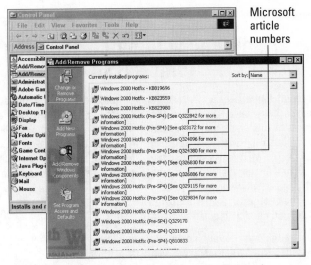

Microsoft article numbers

Figure 9-10: List of installed patches (note the Q article).

3. **In the Uninstall wizard, click Next and answer any questions to remove the patch.**

4. **Reboot your computer.**

   Gotta do it.

Patches usually contain information needed to remove the patch later if needed. However, once in a while Microsoft releases a patch that cannot be removed. I don't know why this is, and I am not going to speculate (in writing). It's just one of those things we have to deal with.

Whoops, end of trail. I hope that you haven't just wound up here, after all this trouble trying to remove a patch, only to discover that the patch you want to remove is permanent. That's why I advise you to read the information carefully before installing a patch.

So what is the remedy if you have to remove a nonremovable patch? Simple. Well, not really: You have to reinstall Windows. Ouch!

Analyzing your patch situation with MBSA

Microsoft has a nifty tool available that you can use to determine the security of your computer. It is called the Microsoft Baseline Security Analyzer, or MBSA. It's not usually mentioned on the Microsoft Security Web page, but if you go to Microsoft's download page or just search for MBSA, you can find it quickly.

Use MBSA to scan your computer only when your Internet access is enabled, as MBSA needs to download up-to-date security information from Microsoft. MBSA will take a minute or two to run, and then it will display a list of patches that need to be installed, as well as other configuration issues it may consider important.

Only make the recommended changes if you understand what the changes will do to your computer. Otherwise you can get yourself into a sticky wicket!

If you are using Windows XP and consider yourself an advanced user, you can back out a patch through the System Restore feature. Whenever changes such as patches are installed on the computer, Windows first creates a Restore Point, and using System Restore you can return your computer to its configuration at that point in time.

System Restore is configured via the control panel. To restore your computer to an earlier time, choose Start⇨All Programs⇨ Accessories⇨System Tools⇨System Restore.

System Restore will not touch your documents — it will only restore Windows files to the earlier time that you specify.

Chapter 10

Using Firewalls and Spyware Blockers

*I*f you have a good antivirus program that you diligently keep updated, your computer is well protected from many threats associated with connecting to the Internet. It would, however, be an overstatement to say that you're safe from *everything* that can go wrong. Worms sniff around your computer to find openings that a firewall can block before the worms can reach your computer.

Several meddlesome companies use a variety of tools and methods to track your movements on the Internet: which Web sites you visit and from which Web sites you purchase goods and services. Some devious Web site operators will even attempt to reconfigure your Web browser to visit their site when you first start your browser or change the page displayed if you mistype a Web site's name. If this concerns you, consider getting one or more antispyware programs.

If, in addition to your antivirus program, you also get a firewall and a spyware blocker, then your computer will have a considerably higher level of protection.

Protecting Your Computer with a Firewall

Windows computers can be attacked in many ways — and not just with viruses, worms, or Trojan horses. Another popular way to attack a Windows computer is to attempt to communicate to it over any of the network *"ports"* found on Windows computers. These ports are kind of like TV channels or radio frequencies: Computers are set up to listen for messages that may arrive from other computers — this is how they communicate with one another.

How firewalls work

Firewalls monitor all the communication between your computer and the Internet. Firewalls know what kinds of communication are allowed to flow in and out. They know this because they have something called an "access control list" — a list of rules that specify precisely what kinds of communications are allowed and what kinds are blocked. The firewalls made for the consumer market (that's us) are usually preconfigured to offer maximum protection right out of the box.

The configuration required to facilitate communication between two computers in a home network makes them *highly vulnerable to attack* from any computer on the Internet. (Sinister music begins to play; the camera zooms in. . . .)

To turn your computer into a tattletale zombie, all anyone on the Internet needs to do is send a specially tailored message from their computer to one of yours — over one of the open ports.

Whether the firewall is a hardware device connected to your network, or a software program in your computer, a firewall will automatically block all unwanted network communication from the Internet, while at the same time permitting any legitimate communication that you need to use your computer. Figure 10-1 shows how a firewall blocks certain communication paths from the Internet.

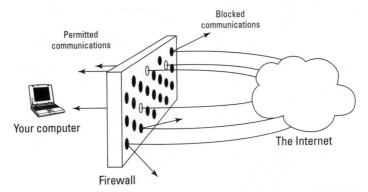

Figure 10-1: A firewall blocks unwanted communication from the Internet.

There are two principal types of firewalls: hardware and software. A hardware firewall is a device connected to the network in such a way that all communications between any computer and the Internet must pass through the firewall and be examined to see whether they should be discarded or allowed to pass through.

A software firewall is a program that runs on a computer and performs the same type of examination of network communications that a hardware firewall does. But where a hardware firewall can protect all of the computers on a network, a software firewall only protects the computer it is running on.

Table 10-1 lists some of the pros and cons of hardware and software firewalls.

Table 10-1	Comparison of Hardware and Software Firewalls	
Issue	*Hardware Firewall*	*Software Firewall*
Protection	All computers on the network	One computer only
Portability	Forget it	Goes everywhere your computer goes

(continued)

Table 10-1 *(continued)*

Issue	Hardware Firewall	Software Firewall
Cost	$40–$200 No freebies	$30–$60 Some are free
Ease of initial setup	Easy to moderate	Easy to moderate
Ease of configuration	Easy to moderate	Easy to moderate
Impact on PC performance	Zero	Negligible
Blinking Lights	Some	None
Available via download	Rarely	Often

Software firewalls

A software firewall is a program that runs inside your computer and blocks unwanted network traffic, as shown in Figure 10-2. Software firewalls are a necessity for any laptop computer, especially one that connects to the Internet from a variety of locations. Wherever your laptop goes, so too goes your firewall, because it's right there inside. But if you have a desktop computer and you connect to the Internet using a dial-up modem, you've got to get a software firewall to protect it.

Sometimes software firewalls are known as *personal firewalls,* so named because they are your very own.

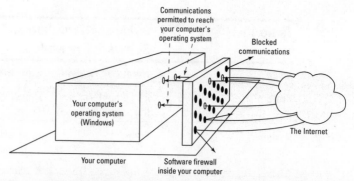

Figure 10-2: A software firewall is a program on your computer that blocks unwanted Internet communications.

Some major antivirus companies have software firewalls in their product families; some of them have all-in-one products that include antivirus, antispam, firewall, and other components. There are also some good software firewall products that have no affiliation with antivirus companies.

Purchasing software firewalls

If you're in the market for antivirus software, or would consider upgrading or switching brands, then I suggest you give all-in-one PC security products serious consideration. Some companies with such offerings include:

- ✓ *Norton Internet Security* **from Symantec:** Included in this bundle are antivirus, firewall, privacy control, antispam, and parental control. www.symantec.com

- ✓ *Internet Security Suite* **from McAfee:** This bundle includes antivirus, firewall, antispam, and privacy control. www.mcafee.com

- ✓ *PC-Cillin Internet Security* **from Trend Micro:** This includes antivirus for your PC and for your PDA, spam-filtering, privacy protection, and antispyware. www.trendmicro.com

Installing and configuring software firewalls

I'm not going to delve into the details on installing the software firewalls included with the big boys like Symantec and McAfee. Instead, I'll tell you about installing and configuring the leading independent (not affiliated with any big and all-powerful antivirus companies) software firewall product, ZoneAlarm, which is available from www.zonelabs.com. Zone Labs has had a free version of their product — which is very good — available for several years. Follow these steps to install and configure this product:

1. **Download the ZoneAlarm setup file from** www.zonelabs.com **and save it on your hard drive.**

2. **Run the download file, which will resemble the name** zlsSetup_45_538.exe.

3. **Answer some installation questions.**

   You're asked a few questions typical of small program installation (location of program files, whether you accept the licensing terms, and so on). Defaults are usually fine.

4. Answer some marketing questions.

ZoneAlarm asks you a few questions about how many computers you have and the speed of your Internet connection. None of these questions has any bearing on ZoneAlarm's configuration.

5. Take the tour.

ZoneAlarm takes you on a little tour. If you haven't used ZoneAlarm, I suggest you take the time to watch the tour, as it will give you useful information about how to set up and use ZoneAlarm.

Was that so hard? Now that ZoneAlarm is installed, there are a few configuration settings to make. Follow these steps:

1. Double-click the ZoneAlarm icon in the system tray.

The ZoneAlarm Control Center opens, in which you can make configuration changes.

2. Click the <u>Overview</u> link; then click the Preferences tab, as shown in Figure 10-3.

3. In the Check for Updates panel, make sure that the Automatically option is selected.

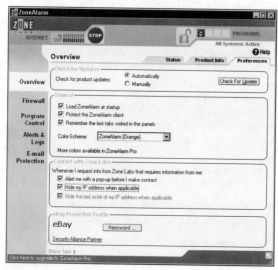

Figure 10-3: ZoneAlarm's Preferences tab in the Overview window.

4. **Click the Check for Update button.**

   Doing so ensures that your ZoneAlarm program can communicate to the Zone Labs update server. If this fails, something is probably wrong with your Internet connection. Time to troubleshoot. First thing: Remove ZoneAlarm. Install it again and see if things are okay. Check its configuration.

5. **In the General panel, ensure that the Load ZoneAlarm at Startup check box and the Protect the ZoneAlarm Client check box are both selected.**

   The Protect the ZoneAlarm Client setting protects the ZoneAlarm program from Trojan horse programs that may try to disable ZoneAlarm.

6. **In the Contact with Zone Labs panel, select the check boxes that read** Alert me with a pop-up before I make contact **and** Hide the last octet of my IP address when applicable.

7. **Click the** <u>Firewall</u> **link; then click the Main tab, as shown in Figure 10-4.**

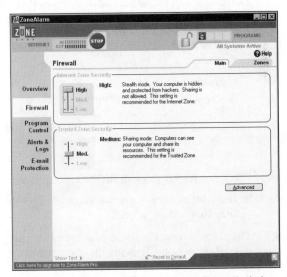

Figure 10-4: ZoneAlarm's Main tab in the Firewall window.

8. **Ensure that the Internet Zone Security level is set to High and that the Trusted Zone Security level is set to Medium.**

   Setting the Internet Zone Security level to High provides maximum protection against hostile threats on the Internet. The Trusted Zone Security level can usually be lower, because this means your computer is protected from other computers in the local network.

9. **Click the <u>Program Control</u> link; then click the Main tab.**

10. **Set the Program Control Security level to Medium.**

    At the Medium level, the first time a program needs to access your local network or the Internet, ZoneAlarm asks you if that program should be allowed to connect. For each program that you use, you will only have to answer this question once, provided you check the Remember This Answer check box.

    The Automatic Lock option can be set to Off or On — I don't care which you choose. I keep mine off. Automatic Lock protects your computer if you stop using it for an extended period of time. You can configure Automatic Lock to activate after a certain period of inactivity, or even when your screen saver is activated.

   The Programs tab of the Program Control window displays a list of all the programs that ZoneAlarm is keeping track of, along with information about which programs are permitted to communicate over the Internet and which are not. The configuration settings for each program are changed in this window.

11. **Click the <u>Alerts & Logs</u> link; then click the Main tab.**

12. **In the Alarm Events Shown panel, select the On option to show all alerts.**

   The Log Viewer tab displays a list of blocked and permitted events. This log can be used to help troubleshoot a communications issue, and it's also gratifying to see all of the attacks that the firewall is blocking.

13. **Click the <u>E-mail Protection</u> link and ensure that the On option is selected in the Basic MailSafe Settings panel.**

Basic MailSafe blocks VBS (Visual Basic Script) attachments in incoming e-mail messages. Frequently, VBS attachments are included in Trojan horse messages that attempt to harm your computer. Basic MailSafe is not configurable in the free version of ZoneAlarm; there are several settings available in Zone Alarm Pro.

Using software firewalls

When they are configured correctly, there is little — if anything — to do on a software firewall. If you're using a software firewall that asks you whether the so-and-so program should be permitted to access the Internet, you'll still see these messages from time to time.

In most cases, you need never look at the logs in which the entries for blocked communications are kept. You're hiring the firewall to keep everyone out, but not necessarily to tell you who they all are.

Make sure that you're apprised of any upgrades in your firewall software. Sometimes flaws are found that need to be fixed, and improvements come along from time to time. To make sure that your firewall software is kept up to date, configure your firewall program to check automatically for updates or add yourself to the firewall company's e-mail distribution list.

With ZoneAlarm and other similar programs, you need to pay close attention to those pop-up dialog boxes that ask if the so-and-so program should be allowed to communicate to the Internet. Viruses and worms that attempt to communicate to other computers will be blocked, *only if you answer "no."* If you don't pay attention and you answer "yes," "yes," "yes" to every program that comes up without reading them, then you may as well not waste your time and money on a firewall.

In addition to ensuring that you have the latest software for your firewall, you also need to familiarize yourself with the way that your firewall tells you whether it's functioning properly or not. Most software firewall programs utilize an easy-to-read status icon in your system tray so that you can quickly check on the status of your firewall.

Your system tray is like a dashboard that quickly tells you the status of your computer. I recommend you *not* configure your system tray to automatically hide itself.

Hardware firewalls

If you have an "always on" Internet connection, then consider using a hardware firewall. A hardware firewall protects all of the computers and other devices on your network, eliminating the need to install a software firewall on each one.

If you're not convinced that you need a firewall, then consider this: fully one third of all personally-owned computers on broadband (cable modem, DSL, and so on) connections have had one or more Trojan horse programs installed and are actively used to relay millions of spam messages and participate in massive distributed denial-of-service attacks. See the sidebar titled "The Legion of Zombies" in Chapter 1 for the horrifying truth.

Hardware firewalls are generally set-it-and-forget-it (or even plug-it-in-and-forget-it) and are very reliable. I have used Netgear and D-Link firewalls (the Netgear firewall was a combination four-port network switch and firewall, the D-Link a combination Wi-Fi network access point, four-port network switch, and firewall), and both were highly reliable. I also use ZoneAlarm on all PCs on my home network, and none has ever detected traffic that the firewalls should have blocked. I have used default settings on both firewall products and have never needed to troubleshoot a problem.

In fact, both hardware firewalls I have used were "plug and play" — all I needed to do was connect them to the network and turn them on, and they began working immediately.

I'm sure that the other major brands of hardware firewalls (which, as I have mentioned, are nearly always bundled with other features such as network switch and wireless network) are as easy to set up and use. However, if you're intimidated by this (or aren't all that sure you can make it work), it may be time to enlist your computer-expert friend again or reach for your copy of *Home Networking For Dummies*.

Selecting and purchasing hardware firewalls

A hardware firewall is a small appliance that you install in your home network. The firewall protects every computer — in fact, anything connected to your network — from the threats present on the Internet.

You can't just buy a *firewall-only* appliance. Instead, many common devices purchased for home networks — switches, routers, and wireless access points — come with a firewall built in. This is a convenience, as nearly all home networks need one or more of these other devices anyway (Figure 10-5 shows where a firewall stands between your home network and the Internet). The most popular hardware devices contain all these functions in one compact unit.

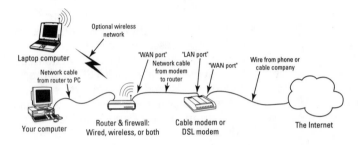

Typical home network with cable/DSL modem, router/firewall, wireless network, and two computers

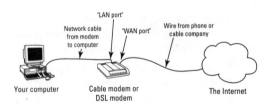

Typical home network with cable/DSL modem and one computer

Figure 10-5: Diagram of a typical home LAN with a firewall in place.

Installing hardware firewalls

There are many different kinds of home networking appliance products that contain firewalls, and many different kinds of home networks. Instead of showing every possible combination of firewall product and home network, I provide a checklist to help you decide what to do:

  ✔ Draw a picture of how your network devices fit together — DSL modem, cable modem, computer(s), anything else, and the wiring that connects them — before you start. If you cannot make the firewall work, you need to put your network back together the way it was before you started.

✔ Label your cables. Same reason.

✔ Write down your computer's network settings before you begin. Follow these instructions to view these settings:

- In Windows 2000, right-click My Network Places, click Properties, right-click Local Area Connection, and click Properties. Find and click TCP/IP in the list of connection types, and click Properties. Write down all of the settings in the General and Advanced windows.

- In Windows XP, right-click My Network Places, click Properties, find and right-click Local Area Connection (found in the LAN section), and click Properties. Find and click TCP/IP in the list of connection types, and click Properties. Write down all of the settings in the General and Alternate Configuration tabs. Don't forget to look at any Advanced settings.

✔ Read the installation instructions that accompany your firewall before you begin. Make sure you understand how to do everything you have to do.

✔ Make sure you have all the necessary cabling. You may need one or more additional "patch cords" (they look like phone cords but have wider connectors).

✔ Make sure you have enough electrical outlets. Your firewall will take up one or more plugs, depending on the shape of your power supply and your plug strip.

✔ Install the firewall in a safe, out-of-the-way location where it will not get spilled on, stepped on, or covered with papers (mine has suffered all of these fates). Make sure it's in a place where you can see the blinking lights.

✔ Be patient. Getting a firewall working should not be too much more difficult than connecting a DVD player to your stereo.

✔ Consider using small adhesive labels (P-Touch or Dymo, for instance) to label your wires and the connectors on your firewall. You may be able to position the labels so that they align with the indicator lights on the front of the firewall so that you can easily see the status of the different ports. It's been my experience that the labels on the firewalls are a bit small, and of course the factory labels don't say "Corinne's Computer" or "Peter's Computer." Well, probably not.

✔ Reward yourself for a job well done. Order a pizza, drink a beer, make love, or take a cruise. (Or have a good read; there are *For Dummies* books to help with all these activities.)

There is one important task to do after your firewall is running. *You must change the firewall's default password!* Read the user's manual carefully and locate the instructions on how to change the password. Use a new password that's easy for you to remember but difficult for others to guess. Write it down in a safe place.

The reason to change the firewall's default password is this: If a security vulnerability is ever discovered in the make and model of firewall that you're using, you could be in trouble if your firewall still has the default password. Hackers know the default passwords for everything, and it could give them access to your network and your computers.

Although serious security vulnerabilities in home firewall appliances are rare, you can't be too careful. Better safe than sorry in all things Internet.

Dealing with Spyware

Viruses are not the only kind of malicious code that can be planted inside of your computer. Spyware, while not exactly (or at least always) malicious, is intrusive to many on account of its goal of tracking or controlling your Internet usage.

In a word, spyware is about *surveillance*. From cookies that track your surfing and buying habits to plug-ins that attempt to hijack your browser to key-loggers that actually record your keystrokes, spyware is trying to find out more about you on every level, and on both sides of the law.

Not to worry. After reading this chapter, you'll know so much about spyware that you can impress your friends and neighbors with your stylish new cloak and dagger — or at least with a spyware-free computer.

Figuring out how spyware invades your privacy

Spyware is a term that applies to a wide variety of features, functions, and bits of software designed for one purpose: to monitor a user's computing habits and send that data back to a central monitoring site. (And you thought there were no "Peeping Toms" on the Internet? Ha!) Spyware uses various methods to track the virtual movements of individuals as they explore the Internet:

- ✔ **Cookies:** Some banner-ad companies (the source of those "banner ads" that appear on many Web sites) use these tiny globs of code to identify your individual system and record what Web sites you visit. The idea is to determine which people are *seeing* which banner ads. This all happens without your clicking a single ad.

- ✔ **ActiveX controls:** Some Web sites or banner ads may attempt to download ActiveX controls into your computer. These are actual programs that can (unbeknownst to you) track your movements, and possibly even capture information such as your e-mail address and *demographics* — gender, age group, geographic region, race, anything that can be used to characterize a targeted group of potential buyers.

- ✔ **Internet Explorer modifications:** Some Web sites — or even HTML-encoded e-mail messages — can attempt to modify certain configuration settings in your Internet Explorer Web browser — for example:

  - Changing the browser's home page (the page displayed when you start the browser or when you click the Home button in the browser toolbar).

  - Changing the Web site that your browser visits if you misspell a URL when you type it in.

  - Adding Web sites to your list of bookmarks.

- ✔ **Surveillance programs:** Whether in the name of national (in)security or crass commercial advantage, nearly anything that *can* be done without your knowledge *will* be done, or at least attempted. For instance. . . .

- **Key loggers:** Some Web sites try to install these programs on your computer to capture your every keystroke and mouse movement — and report them to who-knows-where. For that matter, many viruses *also* attempt to install key loggers on your computer. Something about capturing your bank account numbers and passwords I guess. . . .

- **Screen-capture tools:** These programs "take a picture" of what's on your screen and send a copy along to the (ahem) interested parties.

- **Voice?** Before long, it may be possible to record sounds — after all, many newer computers have built-in microphones — but such instant bugging is still in the realm of science fiction. So far.

These unwelcome visitors generally fall outside the scope of what antivirus programs look for. That means (cue the sinister music) one or more of them may be on your computer now.

Using spyware blockers

Spyware can be detected, blocked, removed, and sometimes even prevented with *spyware blockers*. This section tells you how they work, where to find and install them, and how to use them.

Understanding how spyware blockers work

Spyware blockers check your computer for the existence of spyware components. There are two main ways that these tools work: through whole-computer scans and through real-time detection.

If this sounds similar, it should. These are the two main ways that antivirus programs work.

Spyware blockers watch your computer for things that antivirus programs don't (and if you read the previous section, they'll look familiar):

- **Cookies:** These are the identifiers that Web sites plant on your computer to identify you, whether during a session or between sessions. They make the Web site easier to navigate. They also (in a sense) tag your computer as a known visitor.

✔ **Internet Explorer settings:** Some spyware attempts to hijack your browser by changing your default home page or search settings, and pointing your browser toward their Web sites instead of those you want to visit.

✔ **Downloaded programs:** When you visit some Web sites, they put little supplementary programs on your computer (such as ActiveX and JavaScript). These run on your computer while you're visiting the Web site — and are still on your computer when you log off.

Spyware blockers that watch your computer's activity in real time will block a Web site's attempt to plant a cookie or download a program onto your system. Depending on how you configure it, your spyware blocker may silently block any such trespassers, or tell you when such attempts are being blocked.

Also — like their antivirus cousins — spyware blockers must have up-to-date lists of known spyware on board so they can block (or tell you about) not only the older, well-known spyware components, but also the latest and greatest (or sneakiest and creepiest) spyware. This is done through *signature-file updates* that can occur automatically or be performed manually. (For more on how signature-file updates work, see Chapter 8.)

So, fortunately, using spyware blockers is not all that different from using antivirus programs. Have them run automatically at startup, manually scan once in a while, and get them updated regularly.

Where to find spyware blockers

Because spyware blocking is an emerging technology, there are a few well-established spyware blocker programs, but many, many upstarts and hopefuls. Some good spyware blockers are independents; others are part portfolios of antivirus companies. Personally, I think that by 2005, we'll see market consolidation, mergers, and acquisitions, putting the best spyware blockers into the portfolios of big companies like Symantec, McAfee, Trend Micro, and Computer Associates. And many upstarts will have closed up shop and moved on to something else. (Ah, futurism. Ah, the free market.)

Cookies: Necessary or evil?

There are two types of cookies. Or, more accurately, I should say, two *uses* for cookies. There are *session cookies* and *persistent cookies*.

✔ **Session cookies** are used to identify individual users as they interact with a Web site. For instance, to manage the sessions for several users, an online banking server must be able to positively distinguish one user from another. This is done through cookies. Each time the user clicks a link or pushes a button, the online banking program must first identify which person this is, and then perform whatever steps are required for that person. While it's true that session cookies are not the *only* way to distinguish users, it's a very popular and reliable way to do so.

✔ **Persistent cookies** are used to associate a person's identity from one Web site visit to the next. Like session cookies, persistent cookies provide for a user experience that many people appreciate. The most popular use of persistent cookies is the Web site that "remembers" you from one visit to the next (even if you visit only occasionally), and automatically displays your preferences, customizations, and so forth (zip code, name, colors, and so on).

Persistent cookies are almost universally used to identify users from one visit to the next. Unlike session cookies, where there are a couple of technically feasible alternatives for tracking sessions, persistent cookies are practically the only available means for remembering users between visits.

One common use of persistent cookies is for the tracking of users' Web surfing habits. Most, if not all, big banner-ad companies use persistent cookies when displaying banner ads. Here is an example: The company AdClick displays banner ads on many Web sites. When you visit a Web site, AdClick notes your presence there. Later, when you visit another Web site where AdClick displays banner ads, AdClick notes your presence there, too. Over time, AdClick builds up a history of all the sites you visited where AdClick displays banner ads.

Oh yeah, I'm supposed to tell you where to find spyware blockers. I'll tell you about three reputable, well-known, and effective spyware blockers and where to get them. All three of these are free; some have fee-based "full versions" available that offer additional features (though so far none comes with a crystal ball):

✔ **Ad-aware:** Pioneer and granddaddy of spyware blockers. The free version permits manual scanning only, while the full version provides real-time protection. You can get Ad-aware from www.lavasoft.de.

✔ **Spybot:** Another good program that provides both real-time prevention and system scanning. You can find Spybot at www.safer-networking.org.

✔ **SpywareBlaster:** This program provides real-time detection and prevention. You can get SpywareBlaster from www.javacoolsoftware.com/spywareblaster.html.

In addition to the three sites listed above, these tools are also available from www.download.com.

A corporate lawyer at Wiley Publishing, Inc. (the publisher of these fine books) has reminded me to mention that these spyware blockers are use-at-your-own-risk products and have no formal product support available.

Frankly, I run all three of these programs on every one of the four or five computers I use. I've been using Ad-aware for several years and Spybot for about a year. Between the two, I get pretty good protection and coverage. Recently I have discovered SpywareBlaster; it's nice, complementary, and it concentrates more on prevention than detection.

Many spyware blockers are available, and some may be quite good (others are probably little more than twenty-first-century snake oil). I'm not going to even attempt to function like *Consumer Reports* magazine for spyware blockers, but here's my advice: If you stick with Ad-aware, Spybot, SpywareBlaster, or an antispyware program that's part product portfolio of any major antivirus vendors, you'll be in good shape.

Installing spyware blockers

Installation for Ad-aware, Spybot, and SpywareBlaster are all very straightforward. After you download each program, it's just a matter of running the downloaded program and you're off to the races. I give you some particulars here.

Ad-aware

After you download the Ad-aware installation program, you can run it. Just double-click on the file you downloaded.

Go ahead and click the Next button as many times as needed to proceed through the installation process. The default settings are fine for almost everyone.

Spybot

After downloading the Spybot installation program, you can run it to install the program. Find it with Windows Explorer and double-click its icon.

Click Next as you proceed screen-by-screen with the installation. Be sure to read the license agreement and click the I Accept the Agreement option if you do agree with it. The default installation setting should be fine for you.

SpywareBlaster

Download the installation program and run it.

Click Next to proceed through the installation procedure. Make sure you read the license agreement before you accept it. (The lawyers made me say that. And that.)

After SpywareBlaster has been installed, you can choose to run it right away if you like.

The first time you run SpywareBlaster, you see a Getting Started window that shows you how to perform common tasks such as enabling and disabling protection and downloading updates.

You must activate its protection before SpywareBlaster will protect your computer. If you see the message `Internet Explorer protection is disabled` in the main SpywareBlaster window, then Internet Explorer protection needs to be activated. Follow these steps:

1. **Click the <u>Click here to enable protection</u> link to the right of the message that says** `Internet Explorer protection is disabled.`

   The Internet Explorer Protection window appears, as shown in Figure 10-6.

2. **Select the check boxes that read** `Prevent the installation of ActiveX-based spyware, dialers, etc.` **and** `Prevent spyware/tracking cookies.`

This automatically protects you against all of the known spyware threats, as shown in the list below the check boxes. You *can* examine the list and unprotect yourself from any individual sites if you want, but I wouldn't advise it.

3. **Click the Protect Against Checked Items button at the bottom of the screen.**

4. **Click the Status box at the top of the screen to return to the main Protection screen.**

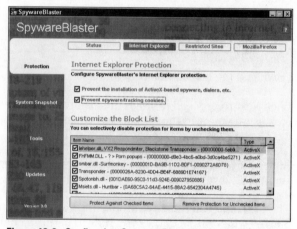

Figure 10-6: Configuring SpywareBlaster's Internet Explorer protection.

Similarly, if you see the message that reads Restricted Sites protection is disabled, activate restriction of sites to protect you against known Web sites that distribute spyware. To do so, follow these steps:

1. **Click the <u>Click here to enable protection</u> link next to the message that says** Restricted Sites protection is disabled.

   The Restricted Sites Protection dialog box opens, as shown in Figure 10-7.

2. **Select the check box that reads** Restrict the actions of spyware/ad/tracking sites in Internet Explorer.

3. **Click the Protect Against Checked Items button at the bottom of the screen.**

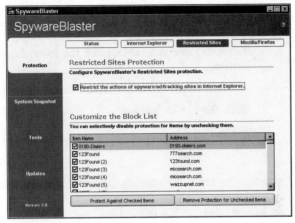

Figure 10-7: Configuring SpywareBlaster to block access to restricted sites.

Updating spyware blocker signatures

Like antivirus programs, spyware blocker programs quickly become ineffective if not regularly updated. The following sections show you how to update signatures for the three spyware blockers I recommend.

Ad-aware

To update the Ad-aware program signatures, follow these steps:

1. **In the main Ad-aware window, click the <u>Check for Updates Now</u> link.**

   The Performing Webupdate dialog box appears, as shown in Figure 10-8.

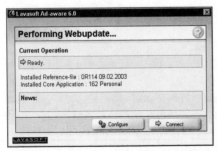

Figure 10-8: Ad-aware is ready to connect and download new signatures.

2. **Click the Connect button.**

   The program tells you whether updates are available.

3. **If updates are available, click the Download Now button.**

   Ad-aware downloads and installs new definitions.

4. **Click the Finish button.**

   You're done!

Spybot

To update Spybot's spyware signatures, follow these steps:

1. **Start the Spybot program.**

2. **Find and click the Search for Updates button.**

   If updates are available, Spybot will display a list of modules that you can download to update Spybot's software and spyware signatures, as shown in Figure 10-9.

3. **Check any updates that are unchecked.**

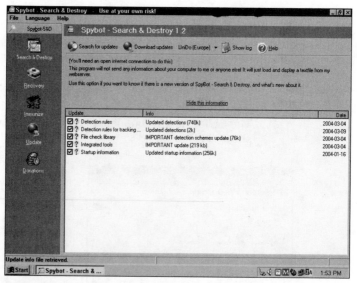

Figure 10-9: Updating Spybot's spyware signatures.

4. **Click the Download Updates button near the top of the Spybot window.**

   After the updates have been downloaded, Spybot will restart itself and you'll see the main menu again.

SpywareBlaster

Follow these steps to update the SpywareBlaster signatures:

1. **Start SpywareBlaster.**

2. **In the main SpywareBlaster window, click the Updates tab on the left side.**

3. **In the SpywareBlaster Updates window, click the Check for Updates button. SpywareBlaster will search for updates, as shown in Figure 10-10.**

   SpywareBlaster checks whether there are newer updates available and downloads them if so.

4. **If new updates were downloaded, click the <u>Enable Protection for All Unprotected Items</u> link.**

Ta-da!

I recommend that you update spyware signatures and scan for spyware no less than once every two weeks. If you have a lot to lose, or you spend a lot of time surfing the Web, you may wish to update and scan as frequently as two or three times each week.

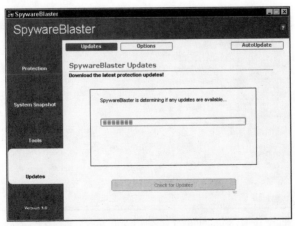

Figure 10-10: Updating SpywareBlaster's spyware signatures.

Using spyware blockers

Just downloading a spyware blocker is not enough, 007. You must *use* it to get the full effect. Just try to bring it back in one piece this time.

Ad-aware

After downloading and updating Ad-aware, you're ready to begin using it. To scan your computer for spyware, follow these steps:

1. **Go ahead and start the Ad-aware program if you haven't already.**

2. **Click the Start button.**

3. **On the Preparing System Scan window, select the Perform Smart System-Scan option, then click the Next button.**

   Ad-aware scans your entire computer for spyware, as shown in Figure 10-11. This could take from 10 to 40 minutes, depending upon the speed of your computer and the size of your hard drive.

   When the scan has completed, Ad-aware tells you how many offending items were found on your computer, as shown in Figure 10-12.

4. **Select the items found. The easiest way to do this is to right-click on one of the items and click the Select All Objects button.**

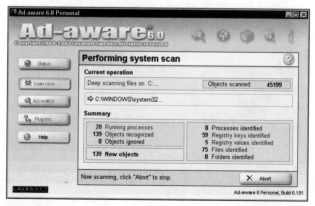

Figure 10-11: Scanning for spyware with Ad-aware.

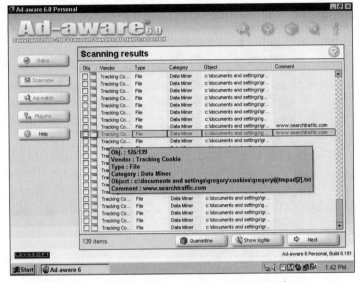

Figure 10-12: Ad-aware captures some sinister fellow travelers.

5. **Click Next; then click OK to remove all the spyware that Ad-Aware found.**

   Ad-aware returns you to the main Ad-aware screen.

Spybot

After you have installed and configured Spybot, follow these steps to scan your computer for spyware:

1. **Start Spybot.**

2. **Click the Check for Problems button.**

   Spybot scans your computer for all the spyware that Spybot knows about and displays the results. The scan will take quite a while, and will show progress at the bottom of the window. You'll see an estimated time remaining at the lower right corner window — I presume it's accurate, but (as the car ads say) "your mileage may vary."

   When the scan has completed, Spybot displays all spyware items it has found, as shown in Figure 10-13.

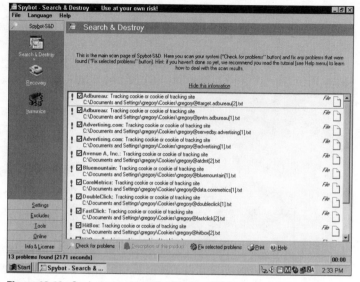

Figure 10-13: Spybot scan has identified lots of spyware in this scan.

If any problems are found, they're displayed in the main window. To view details about any item (see Figure 10-14) select it by clicking the <u>Description of this product</u> link near the bottom of the window.

3. **Click the <u>Fix selected problems</u> link to remove the selected items displayed in the window.**

Figure 10-14: Spybot has committed identified spyware to the deep.

Easy, huh?

You can also configure Spybot to provide real-time protection for your computer, to *prevent* certain problems from occurring. To configure this, follow these instructions:

1. **Click the Immunize button.**

   Doing so brings up the Immunize screen.

2. **In the Permanent Internet Explorer Protection section of the window, click the Immunize button.**

3. **In the Permanently Running Bad Download Blocker for Internet Explorer section of the window, click Install.**

4. **To the left of the Install button, select Ask for Blocking Confirmation so that you can control whether bad downloads should be blocked or not.**

   Then, when you're surfing the Net, if Spybot detects spyware that should be blocked, it will pause and then display a dialog box asking whether the download should be blocked or not.

5. **In the lowermost part of Spybot's Immunize window in the Recommended Miscellaneous Protections section, select the option that reads** `Lock hosts file read-only as protection against hackers` **as well as the option that reads** `Lock IE start page against user changes.`

   If you select the `Lock IE control panel against opening from within IE` option, you won't be able to make any configuration changes in Internet Explorer until you come back to Spybot and uncheck this. However, this does provide the highest protection against any spyware from being able to change the configuration settings in your browser.

SpywareBlaster

There really isn't anything to do to operate SpywareBlaster other than to periodically update its signature. After you configure it, SpywareBlaster watches your computer and blocks all the spyware that it knows about. This is a lot like the real-time protection provided by antivirus programs (for more about that, see Chapter 8).

Chapter 11

Protecting PDAs from Viruses

● ●

In This Chapter
▶ Why antivirus software is needed for PDAs
▶ Installing and configuring antivirus software on PDAs
▶ Protecting your PDA in other ways

● ●

*F*ar from the bumpkins they were long ago, *PDAs* (or personal digital assistants and cell phones with PDA functionality) now sport rich operating systems and *beaucoup* connectivity. PDAs are growing up much like PCs have in the past ten years, although at a much faster clip. The wealth of connectivity options has not gone unnoticed: The era of virus and other attacks against PDAs has begun.

The antivirus companies have responded by offering antivirus software for PDAs. Individuals and large corporations are purchasing antivirus software for PDAs in order to take an early lead against the hackers and virus writers of the world.

PDAs are designed to exchange data freely with PCs, with little attention paid to the information being exchanged. With this in mind, antivirus software for PDAs exists as much to protect the PDA as it does to protect its host PC. Otherwise, the conduit between the PDA and the PC is not guarded as much as it should be.

This chapter tells you more about why you need antivirus software for your PDA, where to find it, as well as other measures you should take to protect your information.

PDAs Grow Up (And Grow Vulnerable)

PDAs can be wonderful tools for people on the go who need instant access to their schedules, contacts, and other information. Early PDAs were little more than electronic calendars and appointment books, so it was difficult — if possible at all — for a virus or Trojan horse to successfully attack a PDA. There was practically nothing *to* attack, and almost no way to *get* there. From a virus's point of view, early PDAs were like a hotel in the middle of nowhere with nothing fun to do.

PDAs are simpletons no longer. They are highly sophisticated devices with rich operating systems and abundant connectivity. Databases and programming languages and other sophisticated applications reside on PDAs. These features are nice to have, but this added functionality comes at a price: Increasingly, PDAs are the likely target of malicious code such as viruses and Trojan horses. While PDAs are not as sophisticated as Windows PCs, they do have some exploitable features that are not well protected.

Because of this increasing vulnerability, many owners of PDAs — as well as the Information Technology managers in corporations — have asked several of the larger antivirus companies to develop antivirus programs for PDAs.

Understanding Why Antivirus Software Is Needed for PDAs

Most big-name PDAs presently available (HP, Sony, Toshiba, Dell, and Blackberry) have operating systems as complex as those found only in personal computers not so many years ago. History has shown us that complexity in computing systems is one factor that leads to exploitation by those whose moral values are (ahem) different from most persons'.

Another factor that leads to the existence of viruses is the widespread adoption of new technology. Computer viruses started showing up in force when PCs were starting to sell in large numbers in the late 1980s. These days, PDAs with the PalmOS and PocketPC operating systems are so popular that exploits such as Trojan horses and viruses are an ever-increasing threat to the mobile platform.

Synchronizing data with PCs

In most instances, PDAs are used as a convenient means of accessing data that usually resides on PCs. Data created on a PC can be copied to its companion PDA, and vice versa — data created on a PDA can be copied to the PC. This process of transferring data is commonly called *synchronization* — and it's potentially one way to use a PDA to attack a PC (or, for that matter, to attack a PDA via a PC).

Surfing the 'Net from a PDA

Wireless technology (or *Wi-Fi*, as it's fashionably known) has enabled PDAs to act as mini-browsers to access the Internet. Directly accessing the Internet exposes a PDA to the many threats that exist there — Web sites with disguised hostile content (meanies that attempt to harm you, your information, or your computer), viruses, scams, and fraud (not to mention those poorly written Web sites that clutter up the screen like cyber-junkshops — but I digress).

Some of you may point out that few, if any, viruses in existence today can directly harm PDAs. Good point — so far. It's unlikely to be true for long, though. I've argued many times that whenever a computing platform such as Windows becomes popular, viruses and other threats are sure to follow. This has held true throughout the Internet age and probably won't change any time soon. Throw a good party and it's an equally good bet that crashers and spoilers will find out — and try to ruin things.

Because I said so

This isn't about royalties, kickbacks, or ego. I just happen to think that the era of using PDAs without antivirus software is drawing to a close.

Well, okay, I wouldn't call you insane if you ran out and purchased a PDA today and *didn't* immediately load it up with antivirus software. But the tide will turn someday; perhaps even as you read this there may have already been more viruses that targeted PocketPC, Palm, Blackberry, or whatever PDAs are in vogue. The more popular PDAs get with customers, the more popular they'll get with virus writers.

Installing and Configuring Antivirus Software on PDAs

Installing software on PDAs is about as simple (or complicated, depending on your point of view) as installing software on PCs. The procedure is about the same, too. For the most part — especially when you're dealing with software produced by the better companies — you actually install the PDA software *on your PC,* and it moves over to the PDA during the synchronization process: As files, e-mail, appointments, and tasks are put in sync between the PC and the PDA, the process automatically pushes the software over to the PDA (where the installation process is completed). Virtually all software installed on PDAs is installed via synchronization.

Configuration of antivirus software on PDAs is far simpler than it is on PCs. This can be done at installation time on the PC — then the configuration is transmitted to the PDA through the synchronization process.

Likewise, you can snag virus-signature updates via the PC and transmit them to the PDA through synchronization. Or, the PDA can perform the virus update directly if it has wireless communications capability.

Protecting Your PDA in Other Ways

There are plenty of things besides antivirus programs that you can do to help protect your PDA and its data. Get ready for several digital hygiene tips — PDA style! As with your PC, the motto "trust no one" will keep your PDA and your information safe. Read on.

Turning off wireless auto-connect

Many PDAs are configured to automatically accept any incoming connection request, whether it's from someone you know or not. If you leave your PDA configured like this, sooner or later you're bound to have someone you don't know connect to your PDA. Is that something you want?

If your PDA communicates using more than one wireless technology (let's see, there's 802.11, Bluetooth, and Infrared, as well as GPRS and 1XRTT if you connect your PDA to the Internet using a digital cellular service such as Cingular or T-Mobile), you probably need to check the configuration for each.

Avoiding ad-hoc wireless network connections

This applies primarily to 802.11 (Wi-Fi) connectivity. You can make two different kinds of connections with Wi-Fi:

✔ **Infrastructure connection:** This is a wireless connection between your PDA or laptop and an *access point* — a designated place built into the network and used for connecting individual devices to a larger network (including the Internet). Such connections can be set up with encryption and other safeguards that protect your communication against eavesdroppers. These are the "good" connections for that reason.

✔ **Ad-hoc connection:** This is a connection between one PDA or laptop and another similar device — used for communicating between the two devices. These connections are often simple and convenient but they have a couple of problems:

  • Encryption of ad-hoc connections is not always available — and an unencrypted wireless connection is a recipe for vulnerability.

  • Some PDAs are set up to automatically accept incoming ad-hoc connection requests — which amounts to opening the door to anybody.

A word to the wise: Unless you rely on ad-hoc Wi-Fi connections (and if you do, you may want to rethink that), turn them off. Doing so saves your battery and keeps your information safe.

Disabling inbound file transfers

Your PDA may be set up to automatically permit someone on the other end of a wireless connection to transmit files to your PDA. Maybe it's me, but I suggest you turn this capability off — or change it to a "prompt" setting where each incoming file transfer requires your permission. Otherwise, who knows what someone might try to load onto your PDA.

Configuring passwords

PDAs are small and disappear easily into a pocket or bag — and not always those of their owners. The last thing you want is for some total stranger to get hold of your PDA and have access to your sensitive data. A number of different protective options are available:

✔ You can configure your PDA to require a password whenever it's turned on — even if you turned it off only seconds ago.

✔ You can configure your PDA to automatically turn off and lock after a short period of time — no more than five minutes. Okay, call me paranoid — but it's *your* data, not mine.

✔ If you routinely use sensitive information on your PDA, you can configure it to periodically require a password *even while you're using it* — and in this case, I advise you to use this option.

✔ Some PDAs require a password to be entered on a PC if you try to synchronize files between the PDA and the PC. You need to enable this feature unless you don't care if someone steals your PDA and can get to your data by connecting it to their own PC.

Your PDA may have other password-protection capabilities. Seriously consider each one in order to protect your data.

People I have spoken with about security often tell me they would rather have convenience than security (sheesh). With

PDAs (and also laptops and anything else that is easily lost or stolen), the person who took your PDA will appreciate the convenience you configured for yourself.

Using secure synchronization settings

Synchronization is the process of transferring information between a PDA and a laptop or desktop computer. You either connect the PDA and the computer with a cable, or connect them using an infrared or wireless connection. Synchronization is usually initiated at the push of a button on either the PDA or the computer, or synchronization can automatically take place at regular intervals. Here are a couple of quick security improvements:

 ✔ **Check whether your PDA can synchronize with *any* PC, or only with *your* PC.** For maximum security, set your PDA to synchronize only with *your* PC.

 ✔ **Set up your PC so that only *your* PDA can synchronize with it.** You don't want your computer getting friendly with someone else's PDA. That would make it way too easy to snatch data out of your PC, or attempt to infect your PC via a PDA.

Avoiding frivolous downloads (or, beware of free programs)

These days, scores of software developers have written programs for PDAs and they're giving 'em away free of charge (the programs, that is). The developers do this to begin to build a customer base and build loyalty. Their long-term objective is to someday charge a fee for people to use their software. I'm straying from my point.

I find it hard to believe that *all* the software available for PDAs is fairly represented. It's a lot likelier that at least a *few* programs currently available for PDAs are actually experiments to test ways of exploiting PDAs or their users. At this stage of the game, it's hard to tell for sure. But as a general rule, stick with the software brand names you know.

Protecting and Securing Your Computer

Say what? Aren't we talking about PDAs?

Yes, that's right. But remember that bad things usually travel from one computer to another — and that includes from PDA to computer, and computer to PDA. Yours. Mine. Anybody's.

PDAs are designed to have regular contact with a computer. Thus, if your computer is clean — free of cyber-infestations — that will help keep your PDA clean.

So it stands to reason: If you run antivirus software on your computer (along the lines I lay out in Part I and Part II), follow all the safe computing practices found in Chapter 12, and sit up straight, you'll automatically keep your PDA safer, too. (Well, okay, sitting up straight is just a good idea. Keeps you alert. . . .)

Chapter 12

Incorporating Safe Computing Practices

• •

In This Chapter

▶ Backing up your data to head off disaster

▶ Using only known, safe programs

▶ Keeping track of licenses and activation codes

▶ Choosing secure Web browser settings

▶ Keeping alternate e-mail accounts

▶ Surfing the Web safely

▶ Taking care with your personal information

▶ Looking at parental Web-surfing blockers

▶ Deflecting spam

▶ Blocking spyware

▶ Using public computers

• •

*P*roperly configured and maintained, antivirus software plays a big role in protecting your computer and your information — but antivirus software can't do it all. There are several other things you need to do to protect your computer and your information.

If everyone with a home computer followed the guidance in this chapter, then viruses, worms, and even spam would not be issues today — at least not the tremendous problems they've become. They got that way largely because most home computers are neglected from a security point of view.

Backing Up Your Data Regularly

Bad things happen to *all* people, not just good people. One of the bad things that happens is data loss — one important file, several files, or everything can disappear into cyber-limbo. Here are some common ways it happens:

- You can simply make some mistake — accidentally deleting data that you can't get back because you already saved over the file, for instance.

- Something can go wrong with your program — an unusual condition that results in your data being changed in a way that you cannot undo.

- An interruption in electric power can cause your data to become corrupted or unusable.

- A malfunction in Windows can cause your data to become corrupted or unusable. Changing a Windows configuration setting or installing a security patch can do this (this is rare).

- The hardware in your computer can fail. Hard drives live only so long, and they usually die suddenly and violently.

- If your data is on a laptop, remember that over 500,000 laptop computers are missing or stolen *every year* in the United States alone. Where is yours, my dear Watson?

- A natural disaster such as a flood, fire, storm, or spilled coffee can damage your computer and the data within it.

- A virus can erase your data or cause a malfunction that results in your data becoming corrupted or unusable.

There are probably more bad things that can happen — these are only a few.

Getting up to speed on backups

I realize — as I am writing this — that *backing up data* is a computer industry term that I learned long ago, but that it's also a habit most folks haven't gotten into yet. I explain it — and answer the question *Why do it?* — here.

Backing up data simply means copying the data from wherever it is to another place. For example, copying data from the hard drive to a CD-ROM, tape backup, or to another computer's hard drive would constitute a viable backup.

Copying data from one place on the hard drive to another place on the same hard drive would *not* be a good backup — if something goes wrong with that one-and-only hard drive, you lose both the original data and the backup data.

As computers began to spring up everywhere, businesses quickly figured out that making backups — up-to-date copies of data on other storage devices — could save much wailing and gnashing of teeth later on. And behold, backups are now a daily ritual in virtually every computer and business facility in the world.

If your data is important to you, then you need to adopt this regular ritual as well. The Grim Data-Reaper visits everyone now and then, and you should be prepared.

Nothing like experiencing data loss spurs resolve never to fail again — and to follow through by regularly backing up important data. I have the scars to prove this point.

Backup tips and strategies

Before I get into how to do backups, I want to share with you some important principles that make them effective. Get these down pat, and your backup routine is more apt to be viable and successful:

✔ **Know where your important data resides:** Whether you create Web sites, write novels, trade stocks online, or run a computer bookkeeping program, you need to know where in your computer the important data lives (*Remember:* By "data" I mean your software and your files). Get the manual out if you have to. If you don't know where your data is, how do you expect to be able to back it up?

✔ **Keep all your important data in one place in your computer:** The invention of the My Documents folder (the folder where most or all the Microsoft programs save files by default) goes a long way toward achieving this consolidation.

✓ **Regularly test your backups:** You've got to make sure that your backups are actually working — that your important data is really being copied to your backup media, *and* that you can actually read your backup media *on another computer*. Believe me, it's worth any amount of trouble to test in advance if you can head off a sorry aftermath.

If you are going to survive a mishap, you'll have to know how to restore your data. You can practice now, or wait until you have a real emergency and then practice under pressure. As they say, *"the best time to fix the roof is when the sun is shining."*

I copy my precious data onto CD-ROM every few days. And once every week or so, I take one of those CD-ROMs and walk it over to another computer to make sure I can actually read it. Why *another* computer? If my main computer "burns to the ground" (a technical term meaning *it stops working for more than several hours*), I'll have to do this anyway.

If you use a special software package to perform backups, then you need to be able to install that package on the computer you will restore your data onto. Backup programs tend to write to backup in a way that is unique from most other backup programs.

Two things generally go wrong with backups:

✓ **Sometimes a backup can be read only on the computer that created it.** This generally is the result of some configuration error, and there's no need to point out that such a backup isn't much good if that computer is toast.

✓ **Sometimes the data you think is being written to the backup media isn't really being written to it at all.** I have heard of companies going out of business because their backups weren't working and nothing was on their backup tapes. Learn from this, please.

Dealing with the Windows backup program

Windows includes its own built-in backup program that you can use to make copies of your data — but you have to configure it if you want to use it. Coming right up. (If you'd like a

full tutorial on how to use Windows Backup, take a look at
Windows 95, 98, or 2000 Registry For Dummies; or *Windows XP
Timesaving Techniques For Dummies.*)

Here's the quick-and-dirty way to run Windows Backup and
get started on the road to regular backups:

1. **Choose Start➪Programs➪Accessories➪System Tools➪
   Backup.**

   The Windows Backup welcome screen appears, showing three tabs and three buttons.

2. **Click the Backup Wizard button.**

   The Backup Wizard starts.

3. **Follow the steps presented by the Backup wizard.**

   The wizard begins by asking you what data should be
   backed up. (Hey, I *told* you that you need to know
   where your data is, right? This is why. You also need
   to specify where the backup should be written.)

Windows Backup likes to write backups to the floppy disk
drive, another hard drive, or a CD-ROM drive. Well, okay,
Windows Backup doesn't *prevent* you from creating a backup
right on the same hard drive where your data is — but c'mon,
you *know* that's a bad idea. A word to the wise: Take the hint
from Windows Backup.

Deciding on third-party backup programs

Sooner or later, if you get frustrated with Windows Backup,
you'll want to take backups to the next level and invest in a
better backup program. There are some really good ones
available — for instance, these:

- ✔ Dantz *Retrospect Backup* is available from www.dantz.com;
  around $130. Backs up to hard drives, CD/DVD drives, or
  tape drives.

- ✔ NovaStor *Novabackup* is available from www.novastor.
  com; around $80. Backs up to CD and DVD drives, SCSI/
  EIDE tape drives, Iomega Zip/Jaz/Click drives, and hard
  drives.

✔ NTI *BackupNow* is available from `www.ntius.com`; around $80. Backs up to CD, DVD, hard drives, MO, Zip and Jaz, and USB jump drives.

✔ Iomega *Automatic Backup* is available from `www.iomega.com`; around $40. Backs up to Iomega Zip drives and Iomega HDD drives. Drag-and-drop restore capability. 30-day free trial available.

All of these products have a 30-day free trial and can be purchased and downloaded online.

Copying files to a CD or DVD

If you have a CD or DVD burner on your computer, it can be a convenient way to back up data, especially if you have a *lot* of data to back up. Who wants to back up a big hard drive to 150 floppies? Not me.

You can use the CD/DVD-creation software that came with your CD or DVD drive (or with your computer), or you can purchase software. Probably the best-known software available is Easy CD Creator 6 from Roxio.

Roxio has a nice wizard (shown in Figure 12-1) to help you select which data you want copied to a CD — again, you must know where your important data resides (see the section "Backup tips and strategies," earlier in this chapter).

You can also use your CD/DVD software to create a new drive letter (for instance, drive D:) to identify the drive that you intend to copy files to. When that's done, you have a couple of options:

✔ Use Windows Explorer to drag and drop files onto the CD/DVD.

✔ Use other programs to save files to the CD/DVD by choosing File➪Save As and then selecting the CD/DVD as the destination.

When you're done with the CD/DVD, right-click and select Eject from the pop-up menu, and the disc-writing software will complete the writing process and eject the disc.

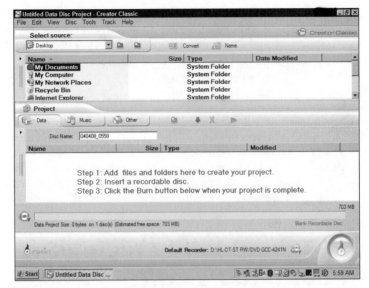

Figure 12-1: Roxio Easy CD Creator makes backups easy.

You can tell Windows Backup to write your backup data to your CD or DVD drive. You can experiment with this if you're the adventurous type.

Copying files to a floppy disk

If your important data files are small (less than about 1.4MB apiece), you can copy them to floppy disk. Follow this procedure to format a floppy disk.

1. **Put the floppy disk in the drive, write enabled.**

2. **Right-click on My Computer and select Explore. A Windows Explorer window opens.**

   The floppy disk drive ("A:") should appear in the right side of the Windows Explorer window.

3. **Right-click on drive A: and select Format.**

4. **Change any options as appropriate (usually the defaults are okay); then click Start.**

   Your PC will format the floppy drive.

5. **When you're all done, press Close, or remove the formatted floppy disk, insert another floppy disk to format, and click Start to begin formatting the next floppy.**

6. **Rinse and repeat.**

That's it! You now have floppy disks that you can copy files to.

 I urge you to keep at least *some* of your backup data well away from the original, preferably hundreds of miles or kilometers away. In my business, we phrase it as *keeping our backup data in a different geographic region* — far enough away that a natural disaster that happens *here* will not also happen *there*.

Installing Only Programs Known to Be Safe

If you're as attached to your data as many of us are, there are two important facts that will probably influence your choice of computer programs:

Not everyone in the world is nice.

That (alas) includes software makers, which leads to another important conclusion:

Not all software can be trusted.

Well, you knew that. Viruses are software, after all, and you certainly can't trust *them* (to do anything good, that is). So unless you really don't care a hoot about your computer and the data on it, the order of the day is to *get reputable software from reputable sources.* Otherwise you're taking your chances — practicing a sort of (ahem) software promiscuity. And if bad things happen then, is it any surprise?

Let me put this into some tips you can use:

✔ Don't get software from spammers, no matter how good the deal may seem to be. They deserve no encouragement (in my opinion).

> ✔ Be very, very careful about software you procure over the Internet, especially if it's from a Web site that you have not heard of.

The more valuable your data, the more stringent you need to be about these principles. If you're making your living with your computer, for example, then you need to be very strict about the data or programs you put into it. Why put your livelihood at risk?

Saving Your License Information

Nearly every time you purchase software — whether you get it from a retail store, have it shipped to you, or purchase a downloadable version — you have to deal with license codes (also called *license keys*) to make the product work. Sometimes license keys come on little stickers in the packaging, other times they are printed on the CD. They might be e-mailed to you, found on a Web page, or even read to you over the phone.

Regardless of how you get your license key and other activation information, you need to keep all this information for all your programs in a very safe place. If you're a hobbyist, it may suffice to put hard copies in a folder in a desk drawer. But if you're making your living using your computer, you had better make copies and keep them in a safety-deposit box or other seriously safe place.

Securing Your Web Browser

Often the security settings in your Web browser are the only defense that stands between you and potentially hostile Web sites. If the settings are too lax, a black-hat Web site can download potentially dangerous and harmful software into your computer without your even knowing it.

You can access the Internet Explorer configuration settings to view or change your security and privacy settings. You can change configuration settings in two sections: the Internet and other Zones settings, and the Privacy settings. The following sections explain these settings in detail.

Internet security zone

The Internet security zone contains all of the security settings that take effect when you visit Web sites on the Internet. Think of the Internet security zone as your standard protection mechanism to guard you from the dangers on the Internet.

To view the security settings in the Internet Explorer Internet security zone, start Internet Explorer and then follow these steps:

1. **Choose Tools⇨Internet Options.**

   The Internet Options dialog box appears, which is a multi-tabbed dialog box.

2. **Click the Security tab.**

   You see the dialog box shown in Figure 12-2, complete with the following four zones:

   - **Internet zone:** This controls IE's actions when you visit Web sites on the Internet.

   - **Local Intranet zone:** This zone controls IE's behavior when you visit internal organization sites. (Normally you see this setting used only in organizations with their own internal Web servers.)

   - **Trusted Sites zone:** Use this zone setting to define which Web sites on the Internet you consider friendly and safe.

   - **Restricted Sites zone:** This zone lists sites that are not trusted at all.

3. **Click the Internet icon to configure settings for the Internet zone.**

   Now, I'm not always a lover of defaults, but I *am* pretty fond of 'em in this context. I think you should have the slider set to Medium or High, but not Medium-Low or Low. Otherwise your browser will trust all Internet sites far more than it should and permit malicious downloads and plug-ins to be installed and run. If you don't see a slider, then your settings have been customized. You can click the Default Level button to revert to default settings and then select Medium or High.

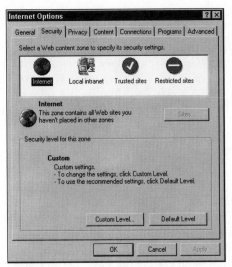

Figure 12-2: The Security tab allows you to change the security settings in IE.

If you want to tinker with the settings yourself, click the Custom Level button. The Security Settings dialog box gives you access to all the individual settings you can tinker with in the Internet Explorer Internet security zone. The precise meaning of all these settings is beyond the scope of this book. If you're baffled by what you see, just click the Cancel button.

Privacy settings

Starting with Internet Explorer Version 6, you have additional control over how your browser handles cookies. If you have IE Version 5.5 or older, then you won't be able to do much with cookie configuration, other than simply to accept all cookies or block all cookies. (I'm assuming you have IE Version 6, which is freely available from Microsoft at www.microsoft.com/ie.)

To adjust your privacy settings in IE, follow these steps:

1. **Choose Tools⇨Internet Options (if the Internet Options dialog box isn't already open).**

2. **Click the Privacy tab.**

   The Privacy tab of the Internet Options dialog box is shown in Figure 12-3. If you have default settings set, you see a slider on the left side of the window.

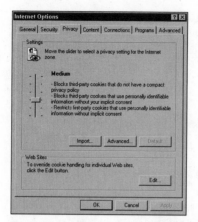

Figure 12-3: Adjusting Internet Explorer to guard your privacy.

I recommend setting the value of the slider to Medium or higher. This setting protects your privacy by allowing only cookies using your personally identifiable information with your consent.

The higher you set the slider, the more trouble you'll have with Web sites that use cookies. Adjust the setting to Block All Cookies and you can forget about doing any online banking, trading, or shopping on the Internet.

If you read the settings that are associated with each security level, you'll soon see that there are many kinds of cookies that have different meanings and uses. You almost have to be a cyber-lawyer to understand what this all means. This is explained in more detail in *Internet Privacy For Dummies*, if you want to be really informed on this complicated topic.

If you don't see a slider, then your privacy settings have been customized. If you like, you can click the Default button, then set the slider to Medium or higher.

If you want to customize your privacy settings, click the Advanced button to display the Advanced Privacy Settings dialog box. You have to hang on for this ride. Here, you can change the way cookies are handled at the security level you're currently looking at.

In Internet Explorer Version 6, you can also control from which sites you will always accept (or always *block*) cookies. On the Privacy tab of the Internet Options dialog box, click the Edit button near the bottom of the window. The Per Site Privacy Actions dialog box opens (as shown in Figure 12-4). That's the box that gives you say-so over which Web sites get to give you cookies — and which ones don't. To specify either, you just type in the URL of the Web site you want to explicitly block or allow in the Address of Web Site field, then press the Block or Allow button.

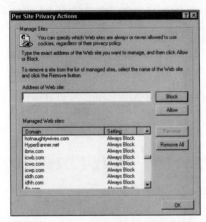

Figure 12-4: IE permits you to block cookies from specific Web sites.

Keeping Alternate E-Mail Accounts

It's more or less inevitable: Over a period of time, many organizations are going to collect your e-mail address. And, sooner or later, after signing up for something and providing your e-mail address to this Web site or that Web site, your e-mail address is going to leak to or be purchased by a mass mailing operator (a nice term for a spammer).

I suggest you get another e-mail account. Use one for corresponding with friends and colleagues, and use another for "commercial" purposes where you have to share an e-mail address with a corporation or other organization.

Surfing the Web Safely

I'm sure that I sound like your mother when I tell you to surf wisely. As soon as you start to venture off the Internet's main street into the dimly-lit back alleys, especially in the red-light district, you'll find a different class of Web-site operator who resorts to dirty tricks like attempting to hijack your browser's configuration settings or burying you in pop-up windows that won't go away until you reboot.

Unless you do have to visit a potpourri of Web sites for (ahem) "research" purposes, I suggest you stay on the paved and well-lit parts of the Internet, where the Web sites have a somewhat better reputation and you're less likely to get into trouble. Even on the Internet, you've got to stay in the nicer and more familiar parts of town. It's especially in the cheesy parts of the Internet where your security and privacy settings work hard to protect you.

Sharing Personal Information Carefully

You need to be careful about sharing personal information about yourself online. By "personal information" I mean things like your name, date of birth, tax identification number, and bank and credit card numbers.

While many sites keep very close tabs on this personal information, other sites don't do such a hot job of protecting *your* information. And one of the other problems is that some of the unscrupulous Web site operators actually sell or give away your private information to others — often (you guessed it) to spammers.

Unless you have no identity, you should seriously consider picking up a copy of *Preventing Identity Theft For Dummies*. And make sure you only purchase it from a truly legitimate Web site, or find it at a bookstore near you.

Adding Parental Internet Blockers

These blockers prevent persons from visiting (deliberately or otherwise) Web sites containing particular content, such as porn, violence, hatred, casino gaming, and Barry Manilow. (Kidding there. I think.)

The main purpose of these products is to protect children from accidentally or deliberately viewing content intended only for adults. They also prevent you from accidentally bumping into unpleasant sites: Try misspelling a Web site's name and see where it takes you. On second thought, don't try it.

Avoiding Spam

Spam is the common name used to describe junk e-mail, or unsolicited commercial e-mail (UCE). Spam is, at the same time, big business for those who create and distribute it and a growing nuisance for its recipients.

By being careful how and where you share your e-mail address, you can help to keep your e-mail address away from spammers' mailing lists. See the earlier section in this chapter, titled "Sharing Personal Information Carefully," for information about the types of information to be leery of giving away.

On the other side of the same coin, you can use a spam blocker to help eliminate the spam you *already* receive. If you're serious about keeping your e-mail address out of the hands of spammers, or if you're already drowning in a sea of spam, get hold of *Fighting Spam For Dummies*. (John and Margaret, you owe me one.)

Blocking Spyware

Spyware is a wide-reaching term that describes software used to monitor your Internet usage patterns, as well as software that can attempt to change your Internet browser configuration, or even record keystrokes (Virginia, the hackers want your bank account and other online passwords).

Most spyware is not malicious in the same way that viruses are, and spyware works differently than viruses do. For this reason, antivirus products do little, if anything, to protect you from spyware. Also, spyware is more of a *privacy* issue than it's a *security* issue.

Antispyware software is used to prevent and/or remove spyware from your computer. Turn to Chapter 10 to take an in-depth look at antispyware tools.

Using Public Computers

Public libraries, Internet cafes, and other customer-serving establishments have their own computers that customers may use to access the Internet. Are these computers safe for you to use?

Tales abound of public-access computers infected with viruses, spyware, and even key loggers, many deliberately planted there in order to elicit information from unsuspecting users. I recall specifically in 2004 a case where a person was arrested for installing a key logger program on a computer in a well-known copy services store in order to record users' bank account numbers and passwords. This is technology gone awry.

Frequently, these computers are configured in a protected manner, so that users can only use a Web browser and nothing else. But, often, you can't even view the browser's security settings, much less change them. So how can you tell if one of these computers is safe? What kinds of things are safe to do on these computers? This section gives you the goods.

Scanning public computers for viruses

In most cases you won't be able to access a public computer's antivirus program to see if its signatures are up to date or to perform a scan. However, you *can* perform one of those online scans that I describe in Chapter 6.

However, if you do find a virus, you may not be able to remove it (many of the online scanning programs only detect — but do not remove — viruses they may find). Better find another computer, but do the establishment (and your fellow customers) a favor and tell them that you have good reason to believe one of their computers has a virus. You may even be decorated as an expert and a hero! Well, if not, you should still feel good after doing your good deed for the day.

Scanning public computers for spyware

It's a good idea to scan a public computer for spyware before you use it. If you use a public-access computer to log into a Web site, particularly one containing financial or personal information (such as a bank), are you willing to bet that the computer is free of spyware?

As of this moment, I'm not aware of online spyware scanners, but there may be one or more available by the time you read this. You can visit my Web site at www.computervirusesbook. com or browse the major antivirus company Web sites to see what's available. It's also possible that one of the current online virus scanners will also scan for spyware. This is a feature that the big antivirus companies will adopt very soon.

Staying clean and cleaning up

Some banking and other Web sites containing your personal information permit you to specify whether you're using a public-access computer. I like to think that in such cases those Web sites prevent your personal information from lingering on the computer for some enterprising busybody to find.

But there are some other things you want to do if you're able. Follow these steps to erase at least some of your tracks:

1. **In Internet Explorer, choose Tools⇨Internet Options.**

   The Internet Options dialog box appears.

2. **Click the General tab (if it's not already in view).**

3. **Click the Delete Cookies button.**

   Click OK if you get an additional dialog box that asks if you want to continue.

4. **Click the Delete Files button.**

5. **In the Delete Files dialog box that appears, select the Delete All Offline Content option; then click OK.**

6. **Click the Clear History button.**

These steps will cover most of your tracks on the computer from prying eyes. The process removes all your cookies, any temporary copies of Web pages you viewed, and the record of the sites you visited. If, however, you are not able to access Internet Options in Internet Explorer, you might consider holding off doing your really personal work until you can get back to *your* computer.

Part IV
Looking at Viruses under the Microscope

The 5th Wave   By Rich Tennant

"Interesting plan. But how do you get him on top of the firewall?"

In this part . . .

*V*iruses don't attack computers. People attack computers. So what is it about the people who write viruses? Their motives vary: Some write viruses because they want to hurt people, as many people as possible. Others want to embarrass Microsoft and teach them a lesson for building such vulnerable software. Some are getting even with a society that cast them aside.

As if the world were bad enough with viruses, there are worms to deal with. Worms are like viruses — they spread from computer to computer and can damage computer software and data. But unlike viruses, which require human intervention to spread, worms can jump from computer to computer all on their own.

Trojan horses are dirty tricks, usually sent in e-mail. They purport to be something they are not, long enough to convince their would-be victims that they should double click the files attached to mail messages.

Then there are the plain old scams, now sent by e-mail. From get-rich-quick schemes to discount prescription drugs to promises of enlarging body parts, there's always someone who wants your money and will try almost anything to get some of it.

Chapter 13

Viruses and the Losers Who Write Them

● ●

In This Chapter

▶ Clarifying what a computer virus is

▶ Tracing how viruses have evolved with the times

▶ Exposing how early viruses spread from computer to computer

▶ Getting inside the heads (yep, we have to go there) of the people who write viruses

▶ Understanding the origins of antivirus tools

● ●

*C*riminal justice investigations often use *profiling* (building a composite of a serial killer by the actions the killer takes) as the sole means of figuring out what the killer's next action may be and who the killer is. Along those same lines, this chapter seeks to bring you into the mind of virus writers and to show you their chosen weapons: viruses.

This chapter brings you up close and personal with viruses, how they got started, and a little bit on how they work. And you'll also see inside the heads of the people who delight in creating and releasing viruses into the world.

Invasion of the Computer Viruses

Simply stated, *a computer virus* is a computer program written by a person (not always, but usually, a *jerk*) who designed it to spread to as many computers as possible.

This definition seems simple enough, but indulge me. I'd like to zero in a bit further, to clarify some issues and to dispel some misunderstandings:

- ✔ **Computer program:** A virus is nothing more than a set of instructions, written in a high-level programming language, such as Visual Basic, C, C++, or Java, translated into "native" instructions (a long list of ones and zeros) that are used by the computer's CPU.

- ✔ **Written:** It's worth repeating: Viruses don't just happen; people write them deliberately. Check out the section titled "The People Who Write Viruses," later in this chapter, for more information about why people write viruses.

- ✔ **Spread:** This is the essential characteristic of viruses. They are designed to be mobile — to move from computer to computer, either under their own accord, or as a "hitchhiker," by attaching themselves to another computer program and then going wherever that computer program goes.

Most viruses also have a *payload,* the instructions that the virus performs in addition to its characteristic of spreading from computer to computer. Consider the payload as the virus's *bonus material.* The payload is usually triggered by some *event,* such as a particular date, a particular time, or a double-click that opens a particular file. The payload can range in behavior — from displaying silly messages on-screen to deleting important files, communicating your personal information to an unknown third party, or sending embarrassing e-mail messages in the name of the computer's rightful user (or, often, some other innocent party that the virus has recently visited, or one found in the victim's e-mail address book).

Trojan horses and worms share many similar characteristics with viruses, although they use slightly different ways to get from here to there. I explain them fully in Chapter 14.

A long time ago in hobby rooms far, far away. . . .

In the early 1980s, several models of personal computers were available. One could go into a store and purchase an

Brain, the first virus

In Pakistan, Basit Farooq Alvi and Amjad Farooq Alvi ran a computer store called Brain Computer Services. They soon discovered that a floppy disk contained computer instructions that were executed when the computer was first turned on. Basit and Amjad used this knowledge for their own purposes and created computer instructions that would change the label of floppy disks in the computer to (C)Brain. The instructions would make a copy of themselves onto other floppy disks that were inserted into the floppy-disk drive.

Brain did nothing other than change a floppy's label and copy itself to other floppies, but that was sufficient to cause trouble. People continued to do what they had been doing for a few years: exchanging computer programs and files using nearly the only available means — circulating them on floppy disks. At first, no one noticed that some of these floppies had a stowaway on board, an unwanted passenger with a single — although relatively benign — purpose.

In 1987, users at the University of Delaware began noticing that the labels on some of their floppy disks were mysteriously being changed to (C)Brain. The Brain virus had made its way from central Asia to North America — and doubtless, to the other continents of the world.

Atari 800, a Tandy TRS-80 (fondly known as the "Trash 80" among the Rubik's Cube generation of computer users), a Texas Instruments TI-99/4, a Commodore 64, or an Apple II. For the first time, computer hobbyists and other curious types could purchase a fully functioning computer system for a relatively modest price.

People were writing and trading programs like crazy, giving one another copies of their programs, pictures, and data files, using whatever portable storage medium their brand of computer used. (The Trash-80 used cassette tapes; others used floppy disks that you could actually flop.) Computer hobbyists and tinkerers were exchanging computer files like school children share colds. Everyone threw caution to the wind.

In the mid-1980s, the most popular personal computer was the IBM PC. The first model had no hard drive — only one (or two!) floppy disk drives. There were soon more IBM PCs — and soon, the clones, like Compaq and others — than all the other popular home computers combined. The first — and most enduring — monoculture was born. The computers that many of us use today are descendants of these legendary beings.

Early viruses get aggressive

Soon after Brain (the first virus), other viruses appeared, such as Jerusalem, Miami, Alameda, Cascade, and Lehigh. These viruses were small sets of computer instructions that covertly implanted themselves somewhere on a floppy disk and could copy themselves from disk to disk.

But unlike Brain, some of these viruses were more harmful. The Jerusalem virus would delete any programs that a person ran on any Friday the 13th. It was named *Jerusalem* because it was first detected at Hebrew University in Israel and was thought to have originated there.

The Alameda virus would copy itself when the computer user pressed Ctrl+Alt+Del (the sequence used in those days to restart the computer). Some descendents (known as "variants") of the Alameda virus on newer PCs with hard drives would erase the contents of the hard drive after the virus had been activated a set number of times.

The Cascade virus had a disrupting, but also humorous, effect. When the virus was activated, the characters on-screen would "fall," piling up in a heap at the bottom of the screen. The result looked funny to just about anybody but the victim (that aspect of prank viruses hasn't changed).

Of course, back in The Old Days™ before Windows, IBM-compatible PCs ran DOS, a "character" environment that could display little more than alphanumeric characters; graphics were crude and mostly non-existent. There were no "windows," no mouse, no World Wide Web, and (as far as most PC users were concerned) no Internet connections. But even then, some people got their kicks from writing programs that worked like biological viruses. The result (shown in Figure 13-1) — even if it doesn't always look like a biological virus — has become as familiar as the common cold.

Figure 13-1: Computer virus, 10,000x magnification.

How Viruses Have Evolved with the Times

Viruses are more sophisticated since they started gaining wide notoriety in the 1980s. When Norton AntiVirus and other tools were successful at detecting and removing viruses from computers, the struggle was on: The people who wrote viruses knew they had to stay one step ahead; they developed ways to make their viruses more difficult to detect.

Encrypted viruses (what a Concept)

The Concept virus was the first *encrypted virus* that tried to hide by storing itself in encrypted form — scrambled so it would not be easily recognized by an antivirus program. Each time Concept was transmitted to another computer, it was re-encrypted using a new *encryption* *key* (the piece of code that later unscrambles the program). Result: Its patterns in the computer changed every time it made a new conquest. This made Concept especialy difficult — at first — for antivirus tools to recognize.

No need to go into niggling detail about the various types of viruses here (unless you want to start a second career writing some of your own — in which case, too bad). But the next sections profile some general ways the little monsters work — in case you want to decide for yourself whether antivirus tools are really worth the money.

How Early Viruses Spread from Computer to Computer

In the mid-to-late 1980s, data was most often transferred from computer to computer by using floppy disks and so-called *bulletin board systems* (BBSs), managed online locations that were the forerunners of today's Web sites.

Stowing away on floppy disks

Even without using the Internet, people in offices where PCs were used traded and circulated programs, documents, and spreadsheets — not to mention jokes, games, filthy pictures, and so forth. The standard method was *sneakernet* — walking up to another person and handing over a floppy disk.

In those early days, viruses spread relatively quickly. Because few people had antivirus programs, there was little to stop a virus from spreading from computer to computer. Like hobos on trains and stowaways on ships, viruses were unwelcome — and mostly unnoticed — passengers that rode for free and left their mark in some way.

Sneaking in via BBSs

Before the World Wide Web, BBSs were the precursors to the way we use the Internet these days. Reached via dial-up modems, BBSs contained a variety of features such as limited e-mail (you could only send messages to other users of that particular BBS), file uploading and downloading, games, and well, bulletin boards (where you could stick any messages you wanted seen by other BBS users), and so forth.

The bug stops here (in the junkyard)

Sometimes obsolescence stops a virus from spreading by stranding it on outmoded equipment or media. For example, I no longer have a computer with a 5¼-inch floppy-disk drive (similar to today's 3½-inch floppy drives, except that the 5¼-inch disks *really were* floppy — and there were also 8-inch floppy disks that were *really* fragile), though I still have a collection of these floppies that contain a variety of programs and files. Some are nearly antique — old (some original) PC-DOS 1.0 and MS-DOS 1.0 & 2.0 boot disks, a Visicalc program disk, and Word 1.0 (made in the days when a single 360*K* floppy disk could contain not only DOS, but also Microsoft Word — and still have room for some documents!). Other floppies contain old documents of mine — and for all I know, one or more of them might contain a virus. But I'll probably never know. I don't have a drive that can read them, haven't seen such drives in computer stores in a long time, and don't want to do any favors for those now-retired virus writers. After all, their creations can only be passed around if the viruses' hiding places can still be accessed. That's one reason they try to infest the newest stuff — and a *great* reason to be really careful about buying used computer equipment.

Modem technology was primitive, with speeds far slower than today's modems. Common modem speeds were 1200, 2400, and 4800 kilobits per second — any faster and the rawhide thongs would break (just kidding) — a mere fraction of the 56000 bits per second (56 kbps) available now. But communication with a BBS consisted of characters only: words, numbers, and punctuation — no graphics. Of course, that also meant no time was wasted loading banner ads, distracting animations, or lame design (any of which can show up on today's Web sites, so the slower modems weren't all that bad).

At the time, going online wasn't all that common, so BBSs attracted users by amassing a rich collection of programs and files — and making those available for download. Often a BBS would award download privileges only to users who had uploaded a certain minimum amount of programs and data, thereby enriching the BBS's collection of goodies. Those file-upload-and-download areas became a big free ride for viruses.

People share stuff

By our very nature, people love to share things. In ancient times, people shared stories, jokes, and other information by word of mouth — and we still do. Native Americans used smoke signals, and early Americans used telegraphs and telegrams to spread funny jokes (surely you don't think it was *all* serious business). Later, when copiers became commonplace in workplaces; people frequently copied jokes, stories, and funny pictures to circulate among their friends and colleagues. People would hand or mail them around among themselves. Companies knew that this eroded productivity and added to copying costs, but people are people, and a reasonable level of this activity was (and is) permitted — or at least not squashed immediately.

As technology marched on, people began using FAX machines and then their computers to spread the jokes, lists, and funny pictures. Some programmers began to write programs that performed tricks or displayed funny pictures on computers, and people copied these and circulated them via floppy disk — and I probably have a few in my dusty collection of floppies. One that I remember would briefly display a picture of a hideous one-eyed monster after about 40 keystrokes or so, but otherwise was harmless. Things like this were modern-day practical jokes and gags.

Today, people use e-mail to circulate funny and interesting items. And you know what? Viruses have advanced with the times and now can spread by e-mail. You can see more about that in this chapter and throughout this book.

Most BBSs had a policy of forbidding the uploading and downloading of commercial software, but it was difficult to police, and BBS operators frequently looked the other way. A number of BBSs did contain illegal copies of commercial software; relatively few perpetrators were caught and prosecuted. But what better lure than something-for-nothing — and hey, how about a little *something extra?* Some of those illegal copies contained (you guessed it) viruses. But I digress.

My point is that viruses would attach themselves to computer programs on a user's system, and if that user uploaded the infected program to a BBS, then anyone who later downloaded and ran that program would subsequently become infected.

As a result, viruses spread faster and over greater distances than they could with floppy disks. Why should an ambitious virus wait for a person to infect one other person at a time in real-world offices (or between friends and among computer-hobbyist club members) when the Internet made *thousands* of potential hosts available? Yum yum.

The People Who Write Viruses

Sometimes I think that it helps to understand a little bit more about the people who perpetrate crimes, in order to be able to avoid being a victim of those crimes. Others of you may just have a morbid curiosity about those who like to hurt other people. Either way, you'll learn a little more about the people who construct the malicious programs that cause billions of dollars of damage each year.

Why they write 'em

The actual crime of writing and distributing viruses is a *crime of anonymity:* The perpetrators usually carry out their crimes anonymously, from the safety of their rooms. They expect never to meet their victims face to face — in fact, they rarely know who their victims are.

Virus writers are, sociologically, not much different from taggers who spray cryptic symbols on walls, or even the "unofficial" graffiti artists: they feel (or *say* they feel) justified in doing their work, and have a wanton disregard for the dignity and property of others. They feel not mere justification, but pride in what they do.

There is an entire counterculture of virus writers, hackers, crackers, and others who compete and try to outdo one another to gain status and respect amongst themselves.

Hackers gather at conventions such as the annual Defcon in Las Vegas. They have "capture the flag" contests — some well publicized, others not. They have clubs with weird names like Cult of the Dead Cow, Cyber Lords, and United Loan Gunmen. Hackers themselves take on equally interesting names like Rain Forest Puppy, Mafiaboy, Sir Dystic, and TeaBag. They even have a couple of magazines, *2600 Magazine* and *Phrack*. You can sometimes find *2600 Magazine* in Borders and other large bookstores.

While I personally have little respect for these persons and their values, I do have a healthy respect for the damage that they can inflict on those who do not know how to protect themselves.

Hacker social values (sort of)

I'm not a sociologist or a specialist in human personalities, but I can venture a few guesses about the values and motives of virus writers and those who help get viruses moving into high gear:

- ✔ **Not much respect for authority:** There's a difference between respect for high-end hacking skills and respect for social institutions; in effect, virus writers seem to respect only themselves. In practice, this amounts to an utter and complete disregard for laws that define their activities as unlawful. Breaking the law becomes a way to rack up bad-boy status. (I use that "bad-boy" term deliberately because most such hackers are males, and hacking is a machismo, alpha-male activity.)

- ✔ **Little respect for the property of others:** An apparent wanton disregard for the information systems that their viruses harm or destroy is shared by virus writers. There's nothing virtual about the real-world effects of cyber-vandalism, however; it's still vandalism.

- ✔ **Little regard for the rights of other people:** Take, for openers, the right to be left in peace. Virus writers seem willing to run roughshod over anyone else to flout authority and show off their skills, usually by destroying the property of others. If they need to satiate a gluttonous desire to witness the wake of the destruction they visit on others' property, it boils down to the ultimate in selfishness — the antithesis of the Golden Rule.

I contend, then, that virus writers lack the basic social and moral values and the "well-formed consciousness" that are the hallmarks of civilized modern societies. Adrift from the civilizations that surrounded them, virus writers seek attention not for productive accomplishments, but for sociopathic, destructive gestures.

In other words, virus writers are (not to put too fine a point on it) a plague. A bunch of losers who write viruses to assert twisted feelings of self-styled superiority over others — while hiding behind anonymity. Some of them even know it — and still won't stop. What remains is for the rest of us to protect ourselves, which brings us to. . . .

The Origins of Antivirus Tools

In 1991, Symantec released the first version of Norton AntiVirus. Norton was a popular brand name among computer technophiles from the well-known and successful Norton Utilities program. Programs like Norton AntiVirus are designed to find and eliminate viruses from a computer, usually with three goals in mind:

- ✔ Make the virus stop doing harm to the computer it has infected
- ✔ Stop the spread of the virus
- ✔ Limit any further harm the virus can do

Early antivirus programs had a database that contained information about each known virus. Chiefly, the database would contain some of the characters that were found in each known virus. Then, as the antivirus program scanned files on the computer, it would simply compare the information in the scanned files with the information about each known virus. When there was a match, the antivirus program had found a virus.

Norton VirusScan was the first antivirus program available. It contained signatures for only several dozen viruses. In those days (reckoned by our sundials and hourglasses) it was sufficient to update signatures every few months. These early programs had no "real-time" detection mechanism; instead, they could only scan a computer to look for viruses that were already present on the computer.

Chapter 14

Trojan Horses, Worms, Spam, and Hoaxes

- -

In This Chapter

▶ Trojan horses: misleading tricks

▶ Phishing scams: skilled imposters

▶ Worms: viruses on autopilot

▶ Hostile Web sites: caution — contains poison

▶ SPAM and viruses: evildoers team up

▶ Scams and fraud

▶ Hoaxes: preying on gullibility

- -

*T*o add insult to injury, viruses are not the only bad things that can happen to you and your computer. The bad guys have cooked up several other forms of malice for us:

✔ **Worms:** These are like viruses in that they spread from computer to computer, wreaking havoc on everything they touch. But unlike viruses, which must attach themselves to another file or program in order to be transported, a worm has its own "propulsion system" built right in. Worms spread amazingly fast through the Internet by scanning for computers that have particular vulnerabilities.

✔ **Trojan horses:** These are destructive programs that masquerade as benign programs. Frequently, Trojan horses arrive in e-mail, where the text in the e-mail message says, for example, "Your e-card has arrived, click here to open." There may, in fact, be an e-card, but to be a Trojan horse the program will also have a destructive characteristic, such as deleting files or corrupting directories.

- ✔ **Phishing scams:** These are sometimes-clever attempts to trick us into giving private information to official-looking (but bogus) Web sites.

- ✔ **Hostile Web sites:** Sometimes these are harmless-looking sites that actually attempt to alter our Web browsers and plant viruses or spyware in our computers.

- ✔ **Internet versions of old scams:** These are plain old scams of every kind — promising everything from body-part enhancement to instant wealth — now marketed (and, sadly, sold) online.

- ✔ **Hoaxes:** These are schemes designed to prey on our trusting nature, either by scaring us with fake virus warnings or tricking us into sending money, information, or e-mail access to the black hats.

Who can you trust anymore? Well, for openers, you can trust me to help you navigate through the darker waters of the Internet that sometimes seem not so far from our front doors. By describing these threats and by showing you a few examples, I hope to give you a leg up on recognizing this filth for what it is — and reliably avoiding it altogether.

Finally — if you have a good antispam program, most (if not all) of this will be filtered out of your incoming e-mail. Having basic protective tools such as antivirus, antispam, and firewall capabilities is much like having The Club: It goes a long way to help keep your car from being stolen, but it's still a good idea to lock your car — and to know how car thieves ply their trade.

Trojan Horses: Misleading Tricks

Okay, sure, Greek mythology glazed some of us over in school, so we missed how *Trojan* applied to the word *horse* — and now people are talking about *Trojan horses in their computers?* What gives? (For a quick refresher, see the upcoming sidebar on "The original Trojan Horse." It *will* be on the exam.)

Identifying a Trojan horse

Trojan horses often arrive as e-mail messages that purport to be something that they are not. They include one or more attached programs that perform some sort of covert and/or destructive act on the information in your computer.

The text portion of a Trojan horse usually contains some sort of message intended to entice the recipient (you) into opening the attachment (the ugly surprise).

Antivirus programs are designed to catch Trojan horses, but knowing that should not lull you into a false sense of security; complacency kills computers. You could be one of the truly unfortunate — early recipients of a brand new Trojan horse that your antivirus program is not yet aware of.

Practicing safe hex

No, it doesn't involve witches' incantations (though some people see hexadecimal code as magic). It's just a geeky way of saying that you need to use your computer safely and responsibly, even if you already have some defensive capabilities such as antivirus programs. As it happens, some safe-hex practices can also help you differentiate a Trojan horse from a legitimate message. Here's a checklist of basic pointers:

✔ Never open mail messages from people you don't know, especially when the subject lines are unfamiliar to you.

✔ Never open mail messages from people you *do* know when the message's subject line is strange, garbled, or nonsensical in an unfunny way.

✔ If you have received a message from someone and you're not sure whether the message is legitimate or not, you should verify the validity of the message *first*, before you open its contents.

✔ Slow down a little. People in a hurry or under pressure make poor judgment calls. If you're going through your e-mail too quickly, you're more apt to open the contents — which can easily be a malicious attachment to a sneaky message — before you have time to think about what you're doing. Such a seemingly minor mistake can have disastrous consequences.

✔ Never open e-mail messages that have no sender listed in the "From:" field. For that matter, messages with no subject line are pretty suspicious too. If you get one of those from someone you know, trash it with out opening it, and e-mail your friend to ask for a re-send with something in the subject line. If your friend didn't send the original message, that will become clear right away.

Those persons who create Trojan horse mail messages have gotten increasingly clever, making it more difficult than ever to distinguish legitimate messages from Trojan horses. In 2003, mail messages containing viruses or Trojan horses contained subject lines such as "Hi," "Hello," and other common and legitimate-sounding subjects. And, oftentimes these messages will claim to have been sent from people you *do* actually know.

How Trojan horses function

Trojan horses, for all the damage they can cause, are really very simple. On the surface, they claim to be something enticing to the recipient, so enticing that the recipient will put caution aside and proceed to open the message's attached file (if, for example, it arrived in e-mail).

When Trojan horse creators build their wares, they know that only a small percentage of recipients will open the message's attachments. It's vitally important that you *not* be in the percentage of suckers who fall for these dirty tricks.

Let me portray for you how a typical Trojan horse program works:

1. **An unsuspecting e-mail recipient (not a reader of this book) is enticed by the text of a message.**

   The sucker, er, I mean *recipient* is so much enamored that he or she opens the attachment, which is a malicious computer program.

2. **The malicious program starts running.**

   If the recipient's computer is running certain brands of firewall or antivirus software, the malicious program may attempt to deactivate them, making the computer vulnerable to other types of attacks.

3. **The recipient, entertained by the "benign" side and unaware of the devious side of this Jeckyll-and-Hyde fiend, may send a copy of the program to his or her acquaintances, thereby perpetuating the little menace.**

4. **On and on it goes, getting a little nudge from each new sucker, er, *recipient* that double-clicks the attachment.**

Eventually, the Trojan horse will be caught by the antivirus companies' traps, enabling the engineers there to dissect the program and create a new signature for it. When they put the signature in their newest signature file, everyone who subsequently downloads the signature file will be protected from that particular Trojan horse.

You know me . . . sure you do . . .

Many Trojan horses are like strangers who arrive disguised as utility workers, law enforcement, or others — who are invited into people's homes. The clever intruder may have even made reference to people the victim knows — because the stranger may have been inside the home(s) of the victim's friend(s) recently. Once inside, they rummage through the victim's belongings, perhaps breaking or moving things around.

This is an official notice . . . sure it is . . .

Here is an interesting case of a Trojan horse. In this example, the mail message claims to be a security update from Microsoft. As Figure 14-1 shows, it looks quite genuine, but it's a fake through and through. A program with an official-sounding name, Q379218.EXE, is attached to this message. Instructions in the message tell the recipient that the attachment is a security update that should be run in order to protect your computer from malicious code. Ironic, isn't it?

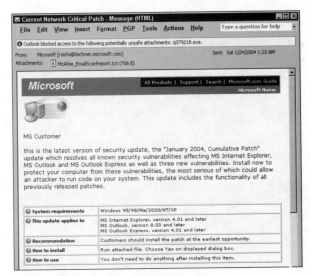

Figure 14-1: Microsoft update? Think again. . . .

In truth, this Trojan horse attempts to disable antivirus programs on the victim's computer, making it vulnerable to later attack.

My own computer had three different defenses for this virus:

1. **Microsoft Outlook blocks attachments that contain program files.**

   So even if I did not have antivirus software at all, Outlook would have blocked it for me.

2. **My antivirus detected and removed the Trojan horse program attached to the mail message.**

3. **Had defenses #1 and #2 failed, my firewall would have blocked the virus from sending messages to other potential victims.**

   The firewall would not, however, stop the virus from doing any damage to my computer, such as changing or removing files. I discuss firewalls in horrific — I mean terrific — detail in Chapter 10.

The original Trojan Horse

The Trojan Horse originated around 1250 B.C. during the war between the Greeks and the city of Troy. The Greeks had laid siege to Troy for ten years, but were unable to defeat the Trojans. The Greeks finally gave up, marched their armies away, and left a giant wooden horse outside the gates of Troy as a parting gift.

The Trojans assumed the giant horse was a tribute from a defeated foe, pulled it inside the gates of their city and began a drunken celebration of their apparent military victory. When the inhabitants of Troy were in a drunken stupor, Greek soldiers who had hidden inside the giant horse emerged and opened the city gates, letting in the Greek army that had sneaked back to Troy — and destroyed the city.

The Trojan Horse became a standard image in legend and literature. Let's see: Something with the appearance of a gift turns out to be a trap that destroys the recipient. There's a lesson in there somewhere . . .

Sure enough, a useful saying arose from this legend: *Beware of Greeks bearing gifts.* The modern counterpart of this saying is, *Beware of geeks bearing gifts.* Another is, *Don't click a gift horse with the mouse.*

Phishing Scams: Skilled Imposters

A *phishing scam* is an attempt to trick a recipient into thinking that a bank or other legitimate business is asking the recipient to verify sensitive information, such as your credit card number, bank account number, password, PIN, and such. The correspondence from the perpetrator appears to be genuine, as well as the Web site that the victim is enticed into viewing. Further, the phishing scam may attempt to take advantage of certain security flaws identified in Microsoft Internet Explorer that cause the browser to incorrectly display the actual web site that the victim is viewing.

You have to hand it to today's scam artists: they are among the most deviously creative persons alive. Take, for chilling example, this actual example of a phishing scam. It all began with a message I received in my e-mail a few weeks ago similar to this one:

```
From: Citibank Service
[mailto:security@citibank.com]
Sent: Thursday, January 29, 2004 10:22 PM
To: *****************.
Subject: Security Update

Dear Citibank Customer,

At Citibank, we value the trust you have placed
in us by using our service to conduct your
transactions. Because our relationship with you
is financial in nature, the protection of your
privacy is particularly important to us.

We are sending this verification notice to
provide you with information about how Citibank
safeguards your privacy, as well as to comply
with U.S. federal privacy guidelines that apply
to financial institutions such as Citibank. The
full terms of Citibank's privacy policy are
available on the Citibank web site, which you
are welcome to review at any time.

Please verify your account information by
clicking on the link below.

Verify your accounts here
```

Gets your attention, doesn't it? And check out those details: This official-looking message shows security@citibank.com as its originating e-mail address — plausible. The language on the message appears to be genuine. And there's just the right note of urgency-and-reassurance *to make you want to click the link.*

No legitimate corporations will ask you to send them sensitive information via e-mail. No bank or credit card company will ever ask you to enter your credit card's PIN on their Web site. It would be like asking you to write your credit-card number on a sticky note and post it in the lobby. The scammers are counting on you not to think about that. Or at least they used to — until enough users got wise.

You can learn more about phishing scams at www.antiphishing.org.

Worms: Viruses on Autopilot

While it's true that viruses and Trojan horses are malicious, there is another threat that's downright diabolical: the Internet worm.

Viruses and Trojan horses require one-on-one human intervention to spread. A virus propagates only when a person executes a program that is infected with the virus. A Trojan horse propagates only when a person forwards it to someone else by e-mail, floppy disk, CD, etc. A *worm* is a different kind of malicious program: Once activated, it takes action by itself — it requires no human intervention to spread. A worm contains all the means necessary to spread from computer to computer with amazing, terrifying speed.

In 2001, for example, the Code Red worm infected over 350,000 servers on the Internet in less than 14 hours. In 2003, the Sapphire/SQL Slammer worm spread worldwide in only 10 minutes, infecting at least 75,000 systems in that time. In 2002, a university researcher described a hypothetical "Flash Worm" which could, if engineered properly, spread to hundreds of thousands of servers in just a minute or two.

We can hope that one stays hypothetical. But I wouldn't bet on it.

Worms are among the most feared phenomenon in large organizations, because they can start without warning and spread so quickly. They can bring a large organization to its knees in less time than even the most adept organization can realize that something is amiss.

How worms function

Worms get around all by themselves — they don't need us. So how do they jump from computer to computer? They travel across the Internet and take advantage of specific weaknesses in the operating systems (usually Windows) running on connected computers.

Your computer is connected to a network — the Internet. Your computer is designed to receive messages on several open "ports" associated with various functions such as e-mail, file sharing, and printing. When messages are received on one of these ports, Windows examines and processes the message.

From time to time, vulnerabilities are discovered in the programs that receive these messages over the network. Sometimes, a hacker can construct specially coded messages that exploit one of these vulnerabilities — sometimes to an extent that gives the hacker control of a victim computer.

Control of the computer means the hacker can cause the computer to do anything he wants it to do — even send these same specially coded messages (called *exploit code*) from the victim computer to other computers.

So a worm has everything it needs to attack and penetrate a computer, and use that computer to send copies of itself to other computers, and so on until no more vulnerable computers can be found. Because human intervention is unnecessary, this can occur even when everyone is watching the Super Bowl.

Defending against worms

As terrifying as worms seem to be, defending against worms is straightforward. The following practices will be quite effective in combating Internet worms.

✔ **Use a hardware or software firewall.** Firewalls will help to repel the network messages that worms send in their search for new victim computers. A firewall that blocks such packets will make the worm believe that your computer does not even exist. Firewalls are discussed in detail in Chapter 10.

✔ **Keep security patches up to date.** Most worms are able to wriggle into your computer by exploiting a known vulnerability in your computer's operating system, Internet Explorer, and other programs. Security patch procedures appear in Chapter 9.

✔ **Keep your antivirus software properly configured and up-to-date.** Should a worm be able to see your computer on the network, your computer's antivirus program will prevent the worm from successfully implanting itself. Antivirus configuration procedures are described in Chapters 5; updating procedures are found in Chapter 8.

✔ **Regularly scan your computer for viruses.** In the unlikely event that a worm has already implanted itself in your computer, a virus scan should root it out and remove it. You can find this information in Chapter 6.

None of these methods by themselves will give you complete protection against worms. But all of these measures together will give you a strong defense in depth that will make your computer practically impenetrable.

Hostile Web Sites: Caution — Contains Poison

Danger seems to come from every direction! Viruses, Trojan horses, worms, high cholesterol, asteroids . . . and now even *Web sites* can be hostile. What's going on here?

Okay, here's the story. Web sites — and Web browsers — have grown amazingly complex. Most of this complexity comes in the form of innovations that permit Web servers to communicate in many new ways with application servers, databases, and users. While a great number of new capabilities have resulted from these innovations, some have security holes that have been discovered.

While innovations in Web technology have brought many new capabilities to the fore, a number of people have used these same innovations to bring harm to you or your computer. Let me explain with a real world example.

Suppose someone who wants to do you some sort of harm sends you an e-mail message, telling you that you should visit a particular Web site. The message that this person sent you is so enticing that — despite your better judgment — you choose to visit the Web site.

When you visit the Web site, malicious code in the Web site is downloaded into your computer and performs some harmful trick. Perhaps it deletes files, plants viruses or a key logger (a program that records your keystrokes and transmits them to a hacker's lair) in your computer, or sends copies of the same e-mail you just received on to other unwitting recipients.

Scary huh? You bet! But, believe it or not, it happens way too often — and it has gotten worse.

Exploits have been discovered in Microsoft Internet Explorer and Outlook that a user can trigger *just by opening an e-mail message*. It's not even an attachment, just an HTML-coded message. Wow!

Can you avoid the damage that malicious Web sites and HTML e-mail messages cause? You can get a start on it by following these principles:

- ✔ Make sure the security settings in your Web browser are adequately protecting you against hostile Web sites. I discuss this in detail in Chapter 12.

- ✔ Keep your antivirus software in good working condition. See Chapters 4 and 5 for more information.

- ✔ Get a spyware blocker. You can find details on spyware blockers in Chapter 10.

- ✔ Avoid visiting Web sites promoted to you by people you don't know, and those that make unrealistic promises. A healthy dose of skepticism goes a long way towards preventing problems.

- ✔ Consider using a spam blocker. You can find more information on spam blockers in Chapter 12.

Your antivirus software will also help, by blocking all *known* viruses from being downloaded into your computer in the first place. But don't be complacent and place *all* your trust in your antivirus program — what if the hostile code is so new that your antivirus software doesn't know about it yet? It's better to act responsibly and safely in the first place. Don't bet the farm on the chance that your antivirus program will always bail you out.

Scams and Fraud

Con artists discovered that the Internet is a useful tool for them to reach thousands — or even millions — of potential victims. Every day I receive dozens of e-mail messages from not-so-nice people who are attempting to defraud me of my hard-earned money. A sampling of topics that scam artists send includes these:

- Discount online pharmacies. They often sell imitations that frequently do not work as promised.

- Medication to increase the size, shape, and/or other characteristics of certain body parts. I've tried all of these and they don't work (I'm just kidding).

- Low rates to refinance a home mortgage. Usually these are bait-and-switch schemes, or even attempts to harvest private information in order to perpetrate identity theft.

- Credit cards with low rates, even for persons with bad or no credit. Ditto on identity theft.

- Elimination of credit-card debt. Ditto again.

- Getting rich on eBay. If this were really possible, why aren't they just doing this themselves and making *all* the money for themselves?

- Getting rich doing practically anything. Ibid.

While many times these messages also contain viruses or enticements to visit Web sites with deliberately harmful content, much of the time these are scam operators who are trying to illicitly obtain some of your private information or sell you something — something that doesn't exist, is illegal, or doesn't do what they claim it does.

Hoaxes: Preying on Gullibility

Perhaps the most interesting kind of malicious content that circulates the Internet is the Hoax. Simply put, a hoax is a message that makes some kind of a statement or a warning that is not true. A hoax contains no malicious computer code like a virus — it just contains words, and perhaps pictures too.

So what's the big deal about hoaxes? Well, some of them have content so enticing or intriguing that people get caught up in them and are seduced into thinking they are real without giving them a chance to consider whether they are genuine or not. Some good examples of hoaxes come to mind:

- **"Beware of the *Good Times* virus."** There was no Good Times virus.

- **"Boy with cancer wants greeting cards."** This one really preyed on our compassion. Trouble is, the boy did not exist.

- **"Bill Gates will pay you to forward this e-mail."** Why would Bill Gates pay *you* to forward a silly e-mail message?

- **"Postal service to levy tax on e-mail."** You guessed it — there was no such pending legislation.

The most skillful hoaxes are those that sound so convincing that they "must" be true (yeah right), and they tug at recipients' emotions to get us to respond quickly before we have a chance to think clearly — and realize that it is (in fact) a hoax.

Strictly speaking, hoaxes aren't harmful aside from the annoyance they cause. And compared to spam, hoaxes don't seem like such a big problem. Still, they waste people's time, and at times they may prompt us to undertake some action that may waste our time or money.

If you get such a message, wait a while before forwarding it to everyone you know. Go to one of the following Web sites to see if the message you received is listed.

- http://hoaxbusters.ciac.org
- http://vil.mcafee.com/hoax.asp
- http://vmyths.com

If the message you did receive is a hoax, you might consider doing what I do: Answer the message with a "Reply All" and tell the recipients that the message is a hoax. Include one or more of the hoax Web sites. This will usually cure many people from sending hoax messages again. Why do you think I never forward hoax messages anymore?

Chapter 15

How Viruses Function and Propagate

• •

• •

*I*t's a fact of online life these days: Viruses just *love* Microsoft Windows. They take advantage of the features and capabilities of Windows, letting Windows itself propel them from place to place. Viruses lurk beneath the surface, occasionally make trouble, and always look for opportunities to multiply and send copies of themselves elsewhere.

This chapter shows you how to identify several kinds of viruses, as well as the various ways they try to stay one step ahead of antivirus programs. And you also get to see how viruses can make the jump from one computer to the next, without having it cost you a hard drive (this time).

One thing is certain: Whenever a new way of moving data from place to place is invented, viruses are sure to take advantage of it. Historically this is true, and don't look for it to change anytime in the near future.

Types of Viruses

To date there are three primary types of viruses that exist today: file-infector viruses, which attach themselves to program files; boot-sector viruses, which install themselves in a hard drive's or floppy disk's boot sector; and macro viruses, which burrow into Microsoft Word and Excel documents. Details on each of these three follow.

File infector

As one of the most popular types of viruses (with the black hats, anyway), a *file-infector* virus arrives embedded or attached to a computer program file — a file with an .EXE extension in its name. When the program runs, the virus instructions are activated along with the original program. The virus carries out the instructions in its code — it could delete or damage files on your computer, attempt to implant itself within other program files on your computer, or do anything else that its creator dreamed up while in a nasty mood.

The presence of a file-infector virus can be detected in two major ways:

✔ **The size of a file may have suspiciously increased.** If a program file is too big for its britches, a virus may account for the extra size. At this point, you need to know two things:

  • What size the file(s) *should* be when fresh from the software maker. You have all of this information written down somewhere, right? (I'm only kidding — I know a lot of "propeller heads" but no one who is *that* cautious.)

  • Whether the virus is a *cavity seeker* — a treacherous type that hides itself in the unused space in a computer program. Clever. Of course, your antivirus program will only know to look for a cavity seeker if. . . .

✔ **The signature of a known virus turns up in an antivirus scan.** The *signature* — a known, characteristic pattern that "fingerprints" a particular virus — is a dead giveaway that a virus is embedded within a program file — provided your antivirus software knows what to look for.

Even if a virus betrays its presence by its behavior, it may not have told you where it's hiding. Sometimes what you need is a special program designed to remove that specific virus. Follow your antivirus program's guidance when it thinks it has found a virus.

Stealth viruses

To stay one step ahead of antivirus programs, virus writers began to incorporate some advanced techniques in their viruses in order to avoid detection. These include

- ✔ **Encryption:** The virus can attempt to scramble its code to avoid detection. Some viruses can rescramble themselves differently each time they're scanned for, so the encrypted code cannot form a part of the virus signature.

- ✔ **Cavity-seeking:** Because an infected file betrays the presence of a virus by being bigger than it should be, some viruses are designed to find — and fit into — leftover space in the files they infect. The idea is to avoid changing the file size, making the virus a little harder to detect. The approach is typical of virus writers who know how antivirus programs work.

You may wonder why there are holes in files. Well, there are some formats of executable programs that enable the programs to load and start more quickly. One characteristic of these formats is the "holes" found in these programs.

Boot sector

While less prevalent today, boot-sector viruses were once the mainstay of computer viruses. A *boot-sector virus* occupies the portion (sector) of a floppy disk or hard drive that the computer first consults when it boots up. The boot sector provides instructions that tell the computer how to start up; the virus tells the computer (in effect), *While you're at it, load me too — before you do anything else.*

Here's the especially devious part: The virus writer knows that after the computer is started, the boot sector isn't used. It's pretty much ignored — the standard tools used to examine a floppy disk or hard drive won't even *look* in the boot sector. Unless antivirus software is used, it's difficult to detect a boot-sector virus. That's partly because the little sweetheart doesn't occupy free space, change the amount of free space available, or change the size of any file on the floppy disk or hard drive. It's pretending to be boot instructions. The only traces of its presence may be (relatively subtle) effects such as excessive hard-drive activity or slowed processing.

Macro

In the early 1990s, Microsoft developed a new capability for documents in programs such as a Word or Excel: These programs could contain computer instructions in addition to their data. After all, if a user had a handy place *in the document* to put tools for working with data — mini-programs called *macros* — a lot of time could be saved. Great idea — but way too convenient. Before long, the usual persons-with-ill-intent figured out how to create document macros with destructive properties.

Windows 95 and Windows 98, the Microsoft operating systems in use at the time, had little in the way of security-access controls. A document macro could carry out practically any operation on the computer without any security mechanism to challenge it — or even record it. Macro viruses are a threat even today; if you've ever seen a warning box crop up to inform you that *This document contains macros,* that's why.

The other name for a macro virus is *Trojan horse* — which makes it a cyber-variation on one of the oldest tricks in any book. (Hint: Think about Greeks bearing gifts and look at Chapter 14.)

How Viruses Propagate

A virus can be successful only if it has a way to propagate from computer to computer. Otherwise, the virus remains only on the computer where it originated, doesn't attract notoriety or vandalize big networks, and is (from its own point of view) a non-event.

Floppies and CD-ROMs

Floppy disks and, later, CD-ROMs and other removable media, were one of the earliest routes for viruses to make the jump from computer to computer. In the 1980s, floppy disks were the primary means for copying data — and viruses — from computer to computer and from person to person.

Typically, files that were already infected with viruses were copied to the removable media and ended up on one or more other computers. File-infector viruses were then activated when the new victim ran the program on the floppy disk or CD. After it's activated, the virus on the new computer carried out its tasks, whatever they were, usually resulting in the virus being implanted in other files on the new victim's computer.

The cycle continued when the new victim, probably unaware that he had a virus, in turn transferred the virus to new victims when he or she put files on floppy disks or CDs for transfer to other people.

File servers

Yep. Even those respectable corporate file servers can harbor viruses. Exchanging computer data by floppies ("sneakernet") has given way to corporate networks with *file servers* — central computers with large amounts of file storage that can be accessed over the company network by all company employees.

Think of it: Instead of running data around on individual disks, one person can copy the data to a specific location on the file server, tell his or her colleagues where to find the data, and (potentially) *everybody* can retrieve the data from the file server. All this takes place over the corporate network with marvelous efficiency.

Consider the possibilities. The virus writers sure have. Some viruses specifically search for file servers in order to install copies of themselves there.

E-mail

The rise in popularity of e-mail in the mid-1990s has provided viruses with a new lease on life. E-mail, and the development of standard means for sending and receiving computer files using attachments, gives viruses a fast track for spreading from computer to computer.

If the virus is to succeed in its mission, usually it has to entice the recipient of the e-mail message to which it's attached. The come-on is usually with some variation on a familiar theme *(open me — it's important, you'll get rich, and/or you know you want to)*. Only when someone opens it can the virus activate and spread. It's like a bomb in a suitcase, set to detonate only if the suitcase is opened — otherwise it's just a suitcase (perhaps heavy, perhaps ticking). A virus in an e-mail message works much like a Trojan horse: The message and its attachment are portrayed as one thing; the message is actually something else. Whoa, that's deep. Chapter 14 provides more information on the differences between viruses, Trojan horses, and worms.

Philosophy aside, viruses that arrive via e-mail are usually spread to other computers the same way. As a rule, after an e-mail-borne virus is activated, it tries to find your e-mail program's personal address book feature (and if you're running an e-mail program that stores addresses on your computer — say, Outlook or Eudora — you have that feature). If the virus finds the address book, it grabs all the addresses and sends copies of itself to some or all of them. Often the mail message sent to those recipients will resemble the same one that arrived in your mailbox, but some viruses have a range of subject lines and messages to pick from — variety is the spice of life, y'know? Even for a virus.

Some recent viruses don't even require the opening of an attachment. Using a hostile version of the HTML code used to build Web pages, they attack the moment the invading e-mail message is opened. The Preview feature in Outlook is no protection; if it's turned on, then the virus may launch at the moment the message is received. It's a classic example of how virus writers are always looking to turn convenience into vulnerability. But there's good news: Newer versions of Outlook have safer security settings and other means for blocking such nasty messages. What version of Outlook are *you* using?

Instant messaging

Instant messaging, or IM, is a relatively new phenomenon that lets people communicate *in real time* over the Internet. IM has similarities to e-mail — you can exchange text messages conveniently with friends — but first-generation IM only allowed messages to pass between users who were online *at the same time.* Messages weren't stored for later retrieval; instead they were displayed on the other person's computer the moment they were sent. If the person you wanted to send an IM message to wasn't online, tough luck. These days some service providers (Yahoo!, for instance) allow offline messages.

Check the metadata

Word and Excel documents contain not only the actual stuff that makes up the document, but also *metadata,* the identifying information about the document — such as who wrote it, who last modified it, and so forth. You can see much of this metadata by opening a document and then choosing File⇨Properties.

Although they are far simpler than e-mail programs, IM programs have had their share of flaws — some of which were originally intended as useful features. For example, IM includes file-transfer capabilities; you can send a file — a document, picture, program file, or (whoops) a virus — to another person. Yep, IM is yet another conduit that viruses can use to get from one computer to another.

Somehow I doubt you're surprised.

In fact, some viruses and Trojan horses have been written specifically with IM in mind. They try to exploit any available flaws in your IM program so they can send themselves on to the next "lucky" recipient, all without your knowledge or consent.

Word and other document types

A macro virus in a Microsoft Word or Excel document has the same capabilities as — in fact, *is* — a virus. It goes back to an attempt (in the late-1990s) to make those documents more useful — and boy, did it ever succeed. People started sending documents to each other like mad, in unprecedented numbers. From the virus's point of view, it was a flood of hitchhiking opportunities — all thanks to the popularity of Microsoft Office programs, coupled with the convenience of e-mailing documents.

A document created in a recent version of Word or Excel also has its own toolkit of *macros* — for example, canned instructions that automatically apply margins to a document or run mathematical functions on designated spreadsheet cells. Some macros are built into the Word or Excel programs; others can be put into the documents themselves so that they are available to other people on their own computers.

Programs inside documents? Uh-oh. . . .

Sure enough, virus writers immediately jumped all over Microsoft's good intentions, twisting the new capability into yet another way to deliver and spread malicious computer instructions. Macro viruses are activated when you open a document that contains a macro virus, and one way that a macro virus spreads is that it can embed itself into other documents on your computer. Then, when you e-mail one of your other documents to someone else, you unknowingly send them the macro virus as well. Nice.

Earlier versions of Word and Excel either had no security controls that controlled macros, or the security controls were turned off by default. More recently, Microsoft has turned this around by turning macros off by default, so even if your antivirus program is not up to date, it's more likely that you would not become infected with a macro virus unless you purposely turn off the safeguards.

If someone has e-mailed you a Word or Excel document, when you see the macro warning, you'll be better off if you *disable* macros, unless you have *no doubt* that the file being sent to you is virus-free. The best thing to do is save the file first, then scan it with your antivirus program.

You can create your own macros by using the macro "Record" feature. This makes it useful to make repetitive steps more automated. But macros can be a good deal more sophisticated than just "tape recordings" of button pushing. Macros can be written in computer languages such as Visual Basic — it is *these* macros that are the real troublemakers.

Web sites

Vulnerabilities in Microsoft Internet Explorer have led to a situation where a cleverly-programmed Web site can actually transfer a malicious program from the Web site to your computer without your consent or your knowledge. Most of the time these malicious programs are contained within ActiveX Controls (another one of those wonderful capabilities that

Microsoft created in order to make it easy for people to exchange nice — and not-so-nice — computer programs among each other).

There are security settings within Internet Explorer that let you control whether you permit Web sites to send ActiveX Controls to your computer or not. Nowadays, the default security settings are tighter than they used to be, but it's still possible for Web sites to download nasty ActiveX Controls with embedded viruses to your computer without your knowing it. And, it's likely that for some time to come this will continue to be an irritating and troublesome security weakness with Internet Explorer. I discuss this subject more fully in Chapter 12.

One problem with these malicious ActiveX Controls centers around exploiting vulnerabilities in Internet Explorer. These flaws can be exploited by creating special coding in the ActiveX Control that can fool Internet Explorer into *trusting* (that is, treating the control as if it's from a trusted source) the ActiveX Control when it shouldn't. It's like someone forging a movie ticket or an airline ticket that could sometimes be good enough to fool the gatekeepers into admitting you when you should be barred from entering.

Newsgroups

Newsgroups — the discussion groups in existence long before the invasion — I mean invention — of the World Wide Web — are a marvelous medium for the distribution of viruses. Newsgroups are like mailboxes where people can deposit articles for everyone else to read. Newsgroup articles rapidly propagate through all the world's newsgroup servers so that anybody reading news anywhere can read all the articles posted there.

Submitting a news article, called *posting,* is very much like writing an e-mail message. Reading a newsgroup article is similar to reading a mail message.

A person intent on harming others can plant viruses and Trojan horses in newsgroups as easily as he or she can in e-mail messages. Then, as people throughout the world read articles from the newsgroup, many may fall victim to the virus. When a person reads an article, the attachment in the article can be opened just as easily as an attachment in an e-mail message. Also, if the news article contains a link to a hostile Web site, then the malicious code in the Web site can do as much damage to the victim as though they received the link through e-mail.

Pirated software

Pirated software is software being distributed illegally, denying the original software maker from the income derived by selling it.

Sometimes viruses can make their way onto pirated software, and for a variety of reasons, including:

- ✔ **Poor quality control:** Often, the distribution of pirated software occurs in sub-standard conditions where viruses may slip in unnoticed.

- ✔ **Deliberate insertion of viruses:** Perhaps the trafficker of pirated software deliberately plants viruses in the software they distribute as a way of inflicting harm on those who purchase the software. You can compare this to a drug dealer who sells tainted drugs to purposely harm his customers.

Wireless networks

There are several forms of wireless networks, each with their own set of risks — some higher than others. In this section I discuss Wi-Fi — the popular home and business wireless network technology — as well as Bluetooth and cellular data networks.

Wi-Fi

Wireless networks in homes and in businesses have become all the rage — they offer the convenience of being able to go online anywhere a signal is present, and the cost of installing a wired network can be eliminated.

Primarily I'm talking about 802.11 networks, also known as Wi-Fi, WLan, 54G, and a few other product names. I'll use the term Wi-Fi from now on.

Some security flaws have been discovered in the 802.11b and 802.11g protocols that Wi-Fi uses, that would permit someone to connect to a Wi-Fi network and eavesdrop on the network traffic. The book *Hacking For Dummies* tells you how to protect your Wi-Fi network from these vulnerabilities. That book would look mighty fine on your bookshelf next to *Computer Viruses For Dummies* (some of your friends might even begin to fear you).

This will continue to be a problem for some time to come, as tens or hundreds of thousands of Wi-Fi access points (for example, the *base stations* installed in homes or businesses) have been sold and deployed. Upgrading all the existing equipment to more secure configurations will be costly and time-consuming — and not everyone who owns one is even aware that there are some risks associated with Wi-Fi networks. And certainly many who know don't understand or care about the risks (I hope that you are not among them).

I advise you to equip each computer in your network with a good software firewall product if you do have a Wi-Fi network. This will practically eliminate the opportunity for a hacker to break in to any of your computers should your Wi-Fi network actually be targeted and successfully broken in to. I talk about firewalls in detail in Chapter 10.

Cellular

Road warriors and others who spend a lot of time "in the field" can stay connected by subscribing to wireless data services offered by most of the larger cellular network carriers. The two technologies generally available are 1XRTT and GPRS, although consumers of these usually encounter friendlier product names such as T-Zones or Mlife.

The risks associated with wireless cellular data networks are substantially lower than with Wi-Fi networks. The encryption of wireless cellular networks has not been broken, and the way that signals are transmitted makes it practically impossible for anyone to eavesdrop on communications.

There *is* a risk that your laptop computer (or PDA, or whatever you're using to connect to a wireless cellular network) could be scanned and compromised. The risks here are very much like the risks associated with connecting to the Internet using a dial-up or high-speed connection: When connected to the Internet (as you are with a wireless cellular connection), you're exposed to scanning and probing by hackers and worms.

The best advice I can give you is — you guessed it — to employ a software firewall. As with Wi-Fi networks, dial-up, and high-speed Internet access, a software firewall provides a nearly impenetrable barrier to anyone or anything that attempts to connect to your computer for nefarious purposes. Turn to Chapter 10 for more information on firewalls.

Bluetooth

Bluetooth network technology is a short-range (up to 30 feet or so) network technology that connects computing devices in a room to one another without the need for wires. The purpose of Bluetooth is not just to eliminate wires between devices, but to provide additional flexibility and computing possibilities not otherwise available or convenient.

You need to be cautious while using Bluetooth; it is only a matter of time before a potentially hazardous flaw is discovered. However, there is still the matter of whether certain connections should be permitted.

Part V
The Part of Tens

"I'm not saying I believe in anything. All I know is since it's been there not a single virus has infected the system."

In this part . . .

"The Part of Tens" is a long-standing *Dummies* tradition. Personally, I've always been fascinated with lists and statistics, and this Part of Tens is packed with cool stuff.

Viruses are misunderstood, so I've started the Part of Tens with ten myths about computer viruses — but one of them is true. Find out the surprising fact about foreign governments.

There are a lot of good antivirus programs. I do an Up Close and Personal with ten of them. Use this list and the associated Web sites to help you make your decision on which antivirus software to trust your computer to.

Chapter 16

Almost Ten Myths about Computer Viruses

*V*iruses are largely misunderstood by most people — including some computer professionals. Here are ten common misconceptions about viruses, and the straight unvarnished truth.

My Computer Stopped — I Must Have a Virus

If your computer stops, it *could* be because of a virus, but I doubt it. Bottom line: It's in a virus's best interest to let the computer continue to operate so the virus can continue to use the computer to spread itself to other computers.

The "best" biological viruses in nature (what a concept) are like this, too. If they kill their host too quickly, there goes their opportunity to spread. A "better" biological virus — like a computer virus — will perhaps just make its host sick, but still well enough to keep spreading the virus.

That said, a virus writer *could* construct a virus that caused severe data damage only after it had been on the computer for an extended period of time. However, there is the risk (to the virus writer) that the virus might be detected and eliminated by antivirus software prior to the time it is programmed to inflict damage.

If *my* computer stopped, I'd suspect hardware or Windows, in that order. I keep my antivirus program, firewalls (hardware *and* software), and antispyware software in good working order, so I'd suspect a virus last of all.

I Have Antivirus Software, So My Computer Can't Get a Virus

Wrong answer. Even with antivirus software, several different factors can still mean that a virus can get in and/or hide in your computer:

- ✔ If you fail to keep your antivirus signatures up to date, then *any new virus* may be able to get inside your computer.

- ✔ If the "real-time" antivirus mechanism in your antivirus software is turned off or deactivated (this can and does happen in the real world from time to time), then the virus can walk right into your computer while the antivirus program is sleeping.

- ✔ A *brand-new* virus can get into your computer even if you keep your antivirus signatures up to date. Remember, it can take a few days or longer for the antivirus software companies to detect, capture, and dissect new viruses before they can update *their* signature files. Even then, your computer will be protected only after it downloads the new signature file from the antivirus software company.

- ✔ If you've been running your computer prior to getting antivirus software and you've put any files on it from any outside source — even if you've never connected to the Internet — there could already be a virus on your computer. If you don't follow the installation procedures and skip the all-computer scan that most antivirus programs want to do when they're first installed, it's possible that a virus that you caught earlier is still be lurking in there.

All Viruses Are Destructive

I disagree with all statements that say *all*. (Well, most of them anyway.) Okay, word games aside, some viruses exist only to replicate themselves, and other than that, they do nothing harmful.

But a purist would say that even these are harmful, because they upset their computers' feng shui. A system with even a benign virus is tainted, and there could someday be some unintended consequence of that.

Bottom line: This one's arguable either way. Wanna have some fun? Get a couple of cyber-philosophers in a room and watch them argue this one for a couple of hours.

Viruses Can Damage Computer Hardware

I know I'm going to get into trouble with this one. Some expert out there is going to have a good counter-argument, but for the most part, this fear is false.

Here's how it looks from the virus writer's perspective: Why aim for the hardware when there's so much brittle software that can be damaged? Go for the easy target first. Besides, if the virus hurts the hardware, how's it going to spread itself any further?

The purist would argue that a virus can damage computer hardware by giving it instructions that make the system misuse some part of itself (for example, by writing excessively to the hard drive), but few such hardware-eating viruses have been released. This is partly because there are so many different types, makers, and formats of computer hardware that one virus would be hard put to trash all of them. Besides, nearly all computer hardware has built-in safeguards that prevent any *real* damage.

But if you *do* get a virus and see sparks or flames shooting out of your computer or keyboard, *please* catch it on video and send it to me.

Viruses Can Hide inside Data Files

Hmmmm, well, this is *theoretically* possible, but I have not heard of such a virus. Yet. For now, viruses hide inside computer *programs* — and in the places where programs normally hang out (such as the boot sector of a floppy disk or a hard drive).

By definition, data files aren't executable, and viruses have to be executed. It's safest to say that viruses hide only in executable program files. But wait. . . .

Macro viruses are found in Word and Excel documents, so if *this* is what you mean by data files, then you're correct. Other than this, generally viruses do *not* live inside data files.

Pictures Can Give You Computer Viruses

Nope. Well, not yet. Pictures are just data files that are read by special programs. But, someday, someone may come up with a picture file format that accommodates the inclusion of computer instructions — for whatever purpose someone dreams up.

Are you thinking "macro virus" right now? So am I. Anytime someone comes up with a way to store data that includes a place for simple computer instructions (like Microsoft Word and Excel do), then the risk of *malicious* instructions becomes a real risk.

I Need More Than One Antivirus Software Program to Be Fully Protected

No, and no. Here's what I mean. As long as you stick with one of the ten or so well-known brands of antivirus programs, you'll find that they all develop new virus signatures at about the same time. So if you're thinking of switching from <Brand A> to <Brand B> because you think that <Brand A> gets their virus definitions out sooner, I personally wouldn't waste my time. For most of us, any of the top ten are fine.

If you're wondering whether this myth means having two different antivirus programs on your computer, don't even try it. Because of the way they work, you can only have one antivirus program running on your computer. Anymore, the antivirus install programs won't even install an antivirus program on a computer if it even *suspects* that there is one there already. The install program is trying to avoid a fight, and you should too.

You Can't Get a Virus from an Official Software CD

I wish. It's rare, but it has happened, and it very well could happen again. The big software companies have very good and almost byte-tight procedures that eliminate the possibility that a virus can sneak into a software development lab and from there to a CD master.

It *can* happen. I wouldn't laugh at you if you scanned CDs for viruses before installing software from them. Promise.

Antivirus Software Companies Create Viruses

To put it kindly, I don't think so. Do the math: The antivirus companies have enough business trying to keep up with viruses "in the wild" that they'd be idiots to risk causing trouble for themselves.

This sounds as crazy as Microsoft and Intel being in cahoots to keep us buying newer computers! Makes an entertaining (if trite) premise for a movie, maybe; doesn't hold up so well in reality.

Some Countries Sponsor Virus Writers and Hackers

Gotcha. This one's actually true. Three or four countries *do* have state-sponsored hackers. I shouldn't name these countries by name, but many of them are known to be hostile to the United States in other ways. Some of these same countries sponsor hackers in order to give us a little trouble.

Official attempts to disrupt and break into foreign information technology go back at least as far as the British code breakers who figured out the Nazi "Enigma" encryption machine in World War II. The adversaries have changed over the years, but their struggle has kept pace with the development of cyberspace, and it continues today.

Chapter 17

Ten Antivirus Programs

*T*here are about three-dozen antivirus programs that you can get for your computer, so listing only ten would not be fair to those that aren't listed.

I don't want this to be a lottery or a popularity contest either. So what I've done instead is list those antivirus programs that you're most likely to find online or in a computer store, for home consumer use.

If you're interested in comparing features a la *Consumer Reports* magazine, then I suggest that you visit cnet.com or antivirus.about.com and locate their reviews for antivirus programs (or for firewalls, antispam, or whatever you're interested in).

Every effort has been made to make the information in this chapter as accurate as possible. However, these fickle vendors are sure to change their Web site addresses and product features (or maybe that's just the nature of technology). Don't blame me!

One thing is certain: Virtually all the antivirus vendors (at least those mentioned here) have moved to the "subscription" model. What this means is that you pay once for the software itself, and with it you have the ability to download virus-definition files for a year. At the end of the first year, you pay a subscription fee to extend your download capability for another year. Typically, the subscription fee is somewhere between 50 and 100 percent of the price you paid for the software.

Command Antivirus

Authentium, the company that sells Command Antivirus, caters to small and big businesses as well as home users. On their home page, just click on the <u>home</u> link (near the bottom-right corner) to purchase online. You can get a description of the antivirus program by clicking the <u>Products</u> link, then clicking Command Antivirus. They have versions for Windows, Linux, Novell, and other systems.

Maker	Authentium, Inc., Jupiter, FL, USA
Web site	www.authentium.com
Free trial version?	Yes, through a sales representative, at www.authentium.com/sales/representatives/index.cfm
Purchase online?	Yes
Available via download?	Yes
Online scan?	Yes, but it's not free (most others are). A free trial is available.
Available for PDAs?	No

Available in a package containing the following?	Firewall: No
	Spam blocker: No
	Pop-up stopper: No
	Privacy protection: No

eTrust EZ Armor

Computer Associates is established as a solid antivirus company for businesses; it's a relatively new antivirus software company for home users. On the Web site, you can ask Sammy a question about viruses or antivirus programs by just typing it in. You can find out about specific viruses and how to configure your antivirus program.

Maker	Computer Associates International, Inc., Islandia, NY, USA
Web site	`www.my-etrust.com`
Free trial version?	Yes, 12 months free trial subscription at `www.my-etrust.com/microsoft`
Purchase online?	Yes
Available via download?	Yes
Online scan?	No
Available for PDAs?	No
Available in a package containing the following?	Firewall: Yes
	Spam blocker: No
	Pop-up stopper: No
	Privacy protection: No

F-Prot for Windows

If I were a virus, I'd be afraid of an antivirus program made by a company named Frisk. Come to think of it, I'd be a little nervous if I was just a program on a computer! What if one of your programs is ticklish?

Frisk has antivirus software not only for Windows, but also for DOS and many popular UNIX systems. They also have a nice alert service that sends you e-mail when virus alerts occur, and also when Frisk upgrades its products.

Maker	Frisk Software International, Reykjavik, Iceland
Web site	www.f-prot.com
Free trial version?	Yes, 30-day free trial
Purchase online?	Yes
Available via download?	Yes
Online scan?	No
Available for PDAs?	No
Available in a package containing the following?	Firewall: No
	Spam blocker: No
	Pop-up stopper: No
	Privacy protection: No

F-Secure

F-Secure has one of the most easily navigated Web sites. The F-Secure antivirus program is available in English, Finnish, Swedish, German, French, and Italian languages. *Togliere il virus per favore!* F-Secure is also available for PDAs that run Pocket PC.

Maker	F-Secure Corporation, Helsinki, Finland
Web site	www.f-secure.com

Free trial version?	6-month free trial at
	`www.f-secure.com/protectyourpc`
	30-day free trial at
	`www.f-secure.com/` `download-purchase`
Purchase online?	Yes
Available via download?	Yes
Online scan?	No
Available for PDAs?	Yes, for PocketPC and Nokia 9200 Communicator
Available in a package containing the following?	Firewall: Yes
	Spam blocker: No
	Pop-up stopper: No
	Privacy protection: No

Kaspersky

These guys look tough. From the looks of the man pictured on the Web site, no virus gets a second chance. Kapow!

They have a nice virus encyclopedia on their Web site too. Kaspersky antivirus software is available in English, French, German, Italian, and Spanish.

Maker	Kaspersky Labs, Moscow, Russia
Web site	`www.kaspersky.com`; Kaspersky also has a nice virus encyclopedia at `www.viruslist.com`.
Free trial version	Yes, 30-day free trial
Purchase online?	Yes
Available via download?	Yes
Online scan?	Yes, at `www.kaspersky.com/` `scanforvirus.html`

Available for PDAs?	Yes, for Pocket PC and Palm
Available in a package containing the following?	Firewall: Yes (firewall offered as separate product)
	Spam blocker: No
	Pop-up stopper: No
	Privacy protection: No

McAfee

McAfee products have been around for years and are still top-quality. They are popular with big businesses and home users alike. There is a Hoax database on the Web site. McAfee VirusScan is available in English, French, German, Italian, and Spanish languages.

Maker	Network Associates, Inc., Santa Clara, CA, USA
Web site	www.mcafee.com
Free trial version?	15-to-30-day free trial available at http://download.mcafee.com/eval/evaluate2.asp?cid=9432
Purchase online?	Yes
Available via download?	Yes
Online scan?	Yes (click link on home page)
Available for PDAs?	No
Available in a package containing the following?	Firewall: Yes
	Spam blocker: Yes
	Pop-up stopper: Yes
	Privacy protection: Yes
	Other: Parental controls: Yes

NOD32 Antivirus System

Here is another solid product with home and corporate editions. NOD32 Antivirus System is also available in German, Portuguese, Czech, Spanish, Italian, and Polish versions.

Maker	Eset Software, Coronado, CA, USA
Web site	www.nod32.com
Free trial version	Yes, 30-day free trial
Purchase online?	Yes
Available via download?	Yes
Online scan?	No
Available for PDAs?	No
Available in a package containing the following?	Firewall: No
	Spam blocker: No
	Pop-up stopper: No
	Privacy protection: No

Norton AntiVirus

Norton AntiVirus was the very first antivirus program for PCs, and it's one of the industry leaders in antivirus software for both home and business use. Their products are consistently solid and reliable. They have one of the most complete suites of computer protection products available.

Maker	Symantec, Cupertino, CA, USA
Web site	www.symantec.com
Free trial version	Yes, 90-day free trial subscription through www.symantec.com/downloads
Purchase online?	Yes

Available via download?	Yes
Online scan?	Yes, at www.symantec.com/securitycheck
Available for PDAs?	Yes
Available in a package containing the following?	Firewall: Yes
	Spam blocker: Yes
	Pop-up stopper: Yes
	Privacy protection: Yes
	Other: Parental controls: Yes

Panda Antivirus Platinum

Headquartered in Bilbao, Spain, Panda has solid antivirus products, and one of the coolest online scanning programs anywhere. Their Internet Security product has many nice features. *Note:* They get my kudos for their social responsibility programs that you can read about online.

Maker	Panda Software, Bilbao, Spain
Web site	www.pandasoftware.com
Free trial version	Yes, 90-day free trial subscription at www.pandasoftware.com/microsoft/english
	30-day free trial from Panda Software
Purchase online?	Yes
Available via download?	Yes
Online scan?	Yes, at www.pandasoftware.com/activescan
Available for PDAs?	No

Available in a package
containing the following? Firewall: Yes

Spam blocker: Yes

Pop-up stopper: No

Privacy protection: Yes

Other: Web-content filtering,
parental control: Yes

PC-Cillin

With this product you actually get a hypodermic syringe and
get to inoculate your computer every week (I'm kidding). The
name does give you a feeling of confidence however.

Trend Micro is a solid player in the corporate space, and
they've been around for years in the home market, too. There
is an online scanner, and a nice, award-winning suite of computer protection products.

Maker	Trend Micro Inc., Tokyo, Japan
Web site	www.trendmicro.com
Free trial version	Yes, 30-day free trial
Purchase online?	Yes
Available via download?	Yes
Online scan?	Yes, at housecall.trendmicro.com
Available for PDAs?	Yes, for Palm, Pocket PC, and EPOC
Available in a package containing the following?	Firewall: Yes
	Spam blocker: Yes
	Pop-up stopper: Yes
	Privacy protection: Yes
	Other: Parental controls: Yes

Vexira Antivirus for Windows

Produced by USA-based Central Command, Vexira is available for Windows and many other types of computers. The illustration on the cover of their boxed product has a man wearing a white lab coat who is holding up a test tube of real computer viruses (would I kid you?).

Maker	Central Command, Inc., Medina, OH, USA
Web site	www.centralcommand.com
Free trial version?	Yes, 30-day free trial
Purchase online?	Yes
Available via download?	Yes
Online scan?	No
Available for PDAs?	No
Available in a package containing the following?	Firewall: No
	Spam blocker: No
	Pop-up stopper: No
	Privacy protection: No

Index